ALPHA MALE

The Alpha Male Bible to becoming legendary and a people magnet. Develop external and internal confidence, charisma, charm & become Sir awesomeness and a winner in life and with women

By

Sir Bruce Wils

Copyright, Legal Notice and Disclaimer

Contents

Chapter 1: Introduction to the Modern Alpha..................9

What is it? What does it mean?..9

The History of Alpha Male 10

The Modern Alpha Male vs the Old Alpha Male 10

Alpha Male vs Beta vs Gamma vs Omega vs Delta vs Sigma..............11

Chapter 2: The Science of Dominance **19**

The Science of Dominance 20

Difference Between Dominance and Prestige 22

Bottomline...24

Chapter 3: The Laws of Manliness..............................**25**

The Laws of Manliness 26

Chapter 4: Characteristics of the Alpha Male **35**

Chapter 5: Developing Your Physical and External Confidence **39**

Fitness..39

Proper Diet 41

Personal Style..43

Grooming..45

Chapter 6: Acting and Communicating Confidently........**47**

Attitude...47

Body Language 49

Verbal Communication...51

Acting Like a Gentleman 54

Handling Criticism...57

Chapter 7: Living Confidently.................................**61**

Happiness 61

Being Likable..62

Trust and Respect 63

5

Handling Self-Doubt 63

Career 65

Chapter 8: Alpha Traits You Should Develop 67

Courageous 67

Easily Controls His Emotions...............................67

Has a Purpose 68

He Makes the Decisions and Stands by Them 68

He is Not Afraid to Speak His Mind 68

He is Not "Governed" by Rules............................. 68

He Keeps Himself Fit 68

Alphas are Not Afraid to Say "No".......................... 68

He is Aware of His Weaknesses and Recognizes Them 69

He has Good Posture.. 69

Chapter 9: The Passionate Alpha.................................71

Chapter 10: Alpha Male – Charisma 75

What Makes an Alpha Male Charismatic? 76

How Charismatic Men Act in Social Situations 76

Golden Rule of Charisma 77

Chapter 11: Alpha Male – Leadership, Lead by Example. 79

Power 80

Influence 81

What Is More Important to Possess, Power or Influence? 82

Chapter 12: Alpha Male Rules of Seduction 83

Create Sexual Tension – Flirt with Her.................. 83

Keep Physically Escalating.................................. 84

Continue Escalating 85

Move-in for a Kiss.. 85

Time to Seal the Deal 86

The Final Escalation.. 86

Chapter 13: Alpha Male with Women 87

Take Charge and Lead... 87

Be Confident 88

Act with Masculine Body Language 88

Lift and Dress Well 88

Be Exciting, Mysterious, and Unpredictable 89

Tease Her Playfully 89

Chapter 14: Alpha Male in Relationship 91

How an Alpha Male Shows Love 91

Chapter 15: How to Be Awesome 95

Examples of Being Awesome..96

Be Awesome 96

Chapter 16: Habits You Should Develop to Become an Alpha Male 99

Conquer Your Fears 99

Don't Let Anyone Tell You What Path to Take...........100

Aim for Constant Progress 100

Don't Argue Just Because 100

Do Good Because it is the Right Thing to Do 101

Always Speak Your Truth 101

Develop Self-Reliance 101

Build a Strong Body 102

You Should Know How to Defend Yourself................102

Take Care of Yourself...102

Live By Your Values 102

Be True to Your Word...103

Master the Art of Charm, Attraction, and Seduction 103

Make Your Life Harder, Taste Sweet Victory Later 104

You Have to be Willing to Die for Something You Believe in.............104

Chapter 17: Secret Tricks that Will Make You More of an Alpha Immediately.. 105

Sound Like an Alpha Male...105

Don't Worry About What Others are Up To 106

Don't Be Passive 106

There is No Comfort Zone – Take Risks.....................106

Be Nice, But Not Too Nice 106
Be Good, But Only When Needed 106
Be Discreet When Giving Praise 107
Never Lash Out When You're Angry 107
Ask for Whatever You Want 107
Love Yourself 107
A Funny Guy is an Attractive Guy 108

Bonus Chapter: The Alpha Checklist 109
The Law of Manliness 109
Characteristics of an Alpha Male................................. 110
Developing Physical and External Confidence 111
Acting and Communicating Confidently.....................111
Living Confidently 112
Character Traits to Develop 112
Develop Charisma 112
How to Be a Good Leader 113
Rules of Seduction... 113
Alpha Male with Women 113
How an Alpha Male Shows Love 114
How to be Awesome 114
Habits to Develop to be an Alpha Male....................... 115
Secret Tricks that Will Make You an Alpha Male Immediately........... 115

Chapter 1: Introduction to the Modern Alpha

What is it? What does it mean?

To better understand what the alpha male really is, let us first know what it is not. The real alpha male doesn't consciously try to dominate his team or community. The real alpha male does not desperately appear to act as an alpha. The one who consciously and desperately tries to be an alpha male lacks the confidence or the integrity to be called one.

Their sense of inadequacy is revealed in different aggressive and disrespectful actions. They would stare down at other people they meet on the streets, hoping to intimidate them. They are loud and quick-tempered not just with strangers or acquaintances but also with their friends. They constantly try hard to prove their manliness with aggression.

This man is not a real alpha male!

The real alpha male is effortlessly charismatic, confident, experienced, physically strong, and successful in everything they do. The real alpha male doesn't feel the need to show off any of their strong characteristics. They are cool. They are calm and collected at all times.

Their presence alone commands respect- they don't need to make people feel inferior for them to respect him. He naturally exudes dominance, without even trying.

Alpha males are "top dogs." In the NBA today, LeBron James was the alpha, the king! in soccer or football, the main man is Lionel Messi of Barcelona. In tennis, Novak Djokovic is number one.

But you don't have to be the best in the world to be considered an alpha male.

The History of Alpha Male

The term *alpha* is the first letter of the Greek alphabet. It is assigned the value of "1" in the same numeric system. Today, *alpha* means a top person:

- Someone who is at the top of the "social chain"

- The strongest

- The boss

- The leader

- The ultimate

- The most powerful

- The supreme

The term "alpha male" (or "alpha female") traces its roots to the 1940s and 1950s. It refers to the highest-ranking male or female.

The Modern Alpha Male vs the Old Alpha Male

These three characteristics embody the traditional idea of what an alpha should be like: *competitive, masculine,* and *dominating*. Part of the old mindset about the characteristics an alpha should possess is the notion of power and glory that comes with being considered one. The old alpha male was perceived to be at the top of the social hierarchy in the animal kingdom, like wolves, gorillas, and lions, as well as in humans. One who has superior strength, superior intelligence, and aggressiveness is seen as an alpha.

For quite a long time, these characteristics are assumed desirable and that alpha males played an important role in societies. Natural-born leaders are these successful males who can easily command power with the use of dominance and aggression.

But these perceived concepts of alpha males have evolved through the years. People started to question the traditional definition of alpha males and rejected the idea of power, politics, the use of superior strength, and aggression as socially normal.

The modern-day alpha male is starting to be seen in the context of generosity, altruism, and diplomacy. They are now finding the right balance between generosity and the use of strength, and diplomacy, and aggression. The modern alpha male is now seen as an improvement of the beta male – one who isn't only an excellent leader but also a good follower.

Alpha Male vs Beta vs Gamma vs Omega vs Delta vs Sigma

Every person is different. Every person is unique. Every person has their own personality traits that make them who they are and provide a reason why they do the things they do. These personality traits are categorized into six: alpha, beta, gamma, omega, delta, and sigma. To better understand men, we have to take a closer look into these six personalities.

Alpha Male

- Confident

  He is naturally confident not just in himself and his abilities, but also with his actions and how he lives his life. He is always confident that he can overcome anything.

  They did not become confident overnight, it took a while to learn to trust themselves and their abilities.

- Outgoing

  His confidence manifests wherever the alpha male goes. He can easily interact with anyone. He remains unperturbed whether he is talking to a powerful man or a woman. He is effortlessly charming.

If he wants to start a conversation with someone, nothing can intimidate him, not even that person's status in society.

His outgoing personality allows him to easily create relationships and social connections.

- A leader

    Whenever someone to lead is needed for a project or at work, the alpha male has no qualms in taking charge and lead.

    They make good leaders because they are effortless in inspiring others and people would willingly follow their lead. They know how to rally a team to work together towards achieving a common goal.

- Charismatic

    The alpha male can easily charm anyone. He just exudes charisma in everything that he does. A charismatic man is like the fictional character James Bond in the movies. They create their own rules.

    An alpha male's charisma radiates that is why people are easily drawn to him. A man who is both outgoing and charismatic is someone a lot of people would like to associate with. They are quite popular because they are fun to be with.

Beta Male

- Friendly

    Betas are no pushover. The beta male is friendly. They respect other people. Friendliness is the most distinguishing characteristic of the beta male. They are kind. With this kind of attitude, they hope to get the approval and admiration of not just their peers, but of everyone.

- Reserved

    This quality often makes people assume that a beta male is shy. He is often unwilling to share his thoughts and opinions. While the beta male is naturally shy, most of them are too intimidated to openly share their thoughts with other people.

Being reserved doesn't mean they lack intelligence or they have nothing to say. They just have limitations on how they can express their thoughts and ideas.

This trait just makes them avoid social interactions most of the time.

- Submissive

Betas frown upon stepping on someone else's toes. The beta male tries to avoid any form of conflict. They try to avoid being on the other end of a disagreement. After all, they will likely avoid defending themselves because they don't want the other person to dislike them.

They avoid expressing opposing opinions because they don't want others not to like them. Some may view submissiveness as something negative. However, there are cases where being submissive is beneficial. For instance, when they have to deal with someone who just wants to create a disagreement or argument, their submissiveness often makes the other person lose interest. This eventually keeps them safe.

- Loyal

One of the biggest strengths of betas is they are extremely loyal. Betas make excellent friends because they will stick with you till the very end.

They also make a good employee because of their loyalty. Betas do not want to cause interruption at work. They may not always speak their mind, but they will never hesitate to take their friends' side when the need arises.

Gamma Male

- Adventurous

Gammas have bits and pieces of the characteristics of all six personality types. They are interesting.

A gamma male creates his own path and doesn't concern himself with the opinion of others towards him.

While the alpha male is perceived to please other people, the gamma male is the opposite. He'll do whatever he wants and he will go wherever life takes him. He finds fulfillment in doing what makes him happy.

The gamma male has his own skills and interests which always give him the desire to explore and enjoy life, to keep on learning, and to do what pleases him.

- Always eager

  He is a man who is determined to get a lot of things in life. He wants to enjoy and experience everything. He is also likely to try new things and always trying to learn new skills.

  They always strive to gain the affection of other people. He may be independent of others, but he is always keen on getting the respect and admiration of other people.

- Always aware

  He is always a stand-out. He is always mindful and aware of his actions and how these actions affect the people around him. This character trait is his ticket to getting far in life.

  Alphas can become a gamma when they become consciously aware of how they act towards other people.

  This trait allows gammas to become well-liked. But they are very independent.

- Empathetic

  Empathy is a character trait that is often associated with females, hence a man being empathetic is both atypical and interesting. Empathy allows a gamma male to understand what others are experiencing. He becomes an effective support system for other people who need to feel supported and understood.

  He is considered to be the most levelheaded of all-male personality.

Omega Male

- Self-assured

  Alphas rely on others to reassure him of his character and status. On the other hand, omegas are the complete opposite.

  An omega male has little regard for how other people see him. This allows the omega male to stay away from insignificant popularity contests.

  An omega man only has a few close friends whom he trusts and respects in his circle. However, his main source of confidence doesn't come from others, but from within him.

This trait becomes negative when the omega male fails to show empathy and care for other people because he only knows how to care for himself.

- Driven

  The omega male possesses an "internal power" that makes him move forward. He always goes after what he wants in life. He doesn't rely on others to cheer him on; in fact, he is his own cheerleader and motivator.

  While other men perform tasks for gratification or reward, omegas are motivated to do something because of their drive to succeed, with or without getting a reward for it.

- Intelligent

  He is the typical "nerdy" man because he is focused on learning and gaining more knowledge. He can easily breeze through complicated algorithms and formulas to crack a code that a lot of people often try to stay away from.

  He tends to listen carefully and make calculated moves and decisions.

  The omega male is seen as a "human calculator".

- Has a variety of interests

  Being nerdy, he is often seen engaged in playing video games, at the same time maintaining obscure hobbies. You'll see him building miniatures and models. His hobbies stimulate the mind.

  He doesn't have a problem with taking on something that most people might not be interested in. He'll always do whatever he wants. He doesn't seek validation from others – he just does things for himself.

Delta Male

- Resigned

  Deltas are a good example of how one's experiences in life can make changes in their personality. Whatever these experiences were, deltas have become more reserved as a result.

  Whether a man went through a bad breakup or a betrayal of someone close to him, he will always have reservations about trusting others again.

- Resentful

  The delta man is full of resentment because of the things he experienced. This also made him distant and calculating when dealing with other people. He will always look for others to blame for his problems, even in situations where he is at fault.

  It is hard for him to move on and will always be resentful towards the person who betrayed him and will constantly use this person so he has someone to blame for his unhappiness.

- Self-sabotaging

  Because he has been out of touch with reality, he doesn't deal with his problems head-on. He continues to live under the illusion that there isn't anything he can do to solve his problems and eventually change his life. He will never acknowledge that he is at fault, and instead, he will continue to blame other people for everything.

  When he is with his circle of friends, he will be manipulative and may even lie just to get what he wants. Because of this attitude, people begin to distance themselves away from him.

  His actions are self-sabotaging as he continues to refuse to trust anyone.

- Lonely

  Bottom line is, he is lonely. His personality may have been different before his sufferings. He might even be an alpha before, with a lot of friends and always the life of the party. But a series of misfortunes, heartaches, problems, and betrayals made him the way he is – lonely, unable to move on, resentful, and skeptical.

  He has hatred in his heart. As he continues living like this, he will become more resentful and he will continue to blame others for it.

Sigma

- Cunning

  While a sigma male is not as powerful or charismatic as an alpha male, he can still easily get away with anything because he is a manipulative and cunning person. You have to be cautious when in the presence of sigma males because they can easily convince you into doing something that you thought nobody can make you do.

They can easily convince people to support their ideas and actions.

- Self-confident

  Someone with a sigma personality is confident, which makes him quite popular, too. But they do not seek approval of others because they are confident in what they can do. These men do not concern themselves with what other people think of them.

  A sigma male doesn't follow rules. He doesn't mind being alone and still feels happy in that aloneness.

- Likable

  A sigma male is likable unless you can see right through his manipulation. He uses his charm to influence people. He is liked by a lot of people because they can see that he is self-confident and doesn't need validation from others to feel good. They are impressed by his strength and power not to follow rules.

  Sigma males often manifest the characteristics of an alpha and an omega. They can get what they want because of their manipulative actions.

- Calculated

  Sigma males make calculated moves. They don't act on impulse. They will often pause and think before responding or reacting to your question. They can always come up with an excuse, either by speaking eloquently or making jokes.

  He is always on guard on his words and actions. He will always come off as witty, smart, and funny, adding to his likability.

Chapter 2: The Science of Dominance

We've learned from the previous chapter the six different personality traits. However, most people know only two categories, the dominant or typically known as a "real man" and the "mister nice guy".

The alpha male is at the top of the social hierarchy; the "real man" who has greater access to money, power, and women, which they easily gain because of their looks, dominance, and intimidation. On the other hand, the beta male is seen as the weaker one, and the more submissive type, or better known as the "nice guy."

This two-way classification is loosely based on observations among other social animals, like wolves and chimpanzees – depicting a clear divide between two "levels" of masculinity. This imposition of only two main categories of the male species in society is misleading the younger male population into acting in predefined ways that do not help find success in all aspects of their life.

It is therefore important to look into the link between these typical alpha male behaviors and attractiveness, and status.

The Science of Dominance

There was a study on the relationship between dominance and attractiveness. Participants were provided with written and videotaped scenarios, and will require them to answer some questions afterwards. Two scenarios are depicted: one dominant and the other is non-dominant.

Here is a snippet of a scenario wherein the man here is depicted as dominant:

"John stands at 5'10 and weighs 165lbs. He has been playing tennis for about a year. He is enrolled in an intermediate tennis class. His returns are powerful. Even with very limited training in tennis, he has won almost 60% of his matches.

His serve is strong and his returns are powerful. He is a competitive player. He is not easily intimidated by better and more experienced players.

Everything about him – his movements and behaviors typically depict dominance and authority. He can easily psyche out his opponents to commit mistakes.

In the second scenario, John is depicted as non-dominant, but still with the same characteristics (as stated in the first paragraph, in italics).

... He is a consistent player – serves and returns are strategically placed. He plays well but he doesn't play competitively. He tends to yield to more experienced players. He easily gets intimidated by stronger players. He easily gets thrown off his game. He is easily psyched out, causing him to lose focus. He does enjoy the game."

Participants were asked who they are most sexually attracted to and most of them answered that they are leaning towards the dominant man. However, they all agree that he is less likable and they wouldn't consider him as spouse material.

At face value, this study supports the idea that the dominant alpha male is more attractive than the submissive beta male.

But that is not actually the case.

In another study, researchers isolated a variety of adjectives that can be considered sexually attractive. Participants considered "dominance" as sexually attractive, while "domineering" and "aggressive" do not appeal to them at all.

In another study where 118 females took part. Participants were asked to read the descriptions of John, the tennis player (the dominant versus submissive). But they included another group, a control condition where the participants were asked to read only the first paragraph of the description (see italics above).

True enough, consistent with the prior study, women were more sexually attracted to dominant John than submissive John.

For those in the control condition, dominant John received a high sexiness rating.

What's going on?

This study doesn't mean that John is attractive only based on the short first paragraph description. Rather, women will find John less attractive after reading about his dominant or non-dominant behavior.

Researchers conclude that a simple dominant vs. non-dominant dimension can be limiting when predicting what women find sexually appealing.

The researchers then played with the descriptors about John.

In the dominant condition, the original set of participants were given a short description of John. They were told that in the recent personality test taken by John, five prominent traits stood out: *assertive, aggressive, demanding, dominant,* and *confident.*

For the nondominant John, participants were given the list of his five most prominent characteristics: *shy, quiet, easygoing, submissive,* and *sensitive.*

Those in the control condition were only asked to read the description but were not given a list of characteristics.

When participants were then asked to identify which of the characteristics best depict John as an ideal date or as a lifetime partner, researchers found that one out of the 50 women in the sample mentioned *"dominant"* as one of the character traits they are looking for in a romantic partner.

As for the rest, the top two were *"confident"* (74% as a romantic partner, 72% as an ideal date), and *"assertive"* (36% as a romantic partner, 48% as an ideal date). No one voted for a *"demanding"* partner, while 12% said they wanted someone *"aggressive"* to go on a date with or even be a romantic partner.

As for the non-dominant characteristics, the top two were *"easygoing"* (68% ideal date, 64% romantic partner), and *"sensitive"* (76% ideal date, and romantic partner). No one said they wanted a *"submissive"* man to date or for romance. The "*shy*" character trait got 2% as ideal date, 0% romantic partner. "*Quiet*" got 4% for an ideal date, 2% romantic partner.

This study suggests that dominance may be seen in different forms. Women are NOT attracted to a dominant, demanding, self-centered, and violent man. Women are more likely to notice a dominant, assertive, and confident man.

This only shows that those men who are dominant because of their leadership qualities and who can provide for their families are considered more attractive than those who have far less superior attributes.

The results also show that sensitivity and assertiveness are not seen as opposites. Further studies suggest that kindness and assertiveness could be the most desirable pairing.

Dominance combined with pro-social behaviors make men appealing to women. This means that dominance only enhances attraction when the man already has more positive characteristics.

Another observation worth mentioning is that women found dominance attractive only when seen in the context of male-to-male competitions. Women are turned off by men who use aggressive dominance (by use of force or threat) when competing for leadership. This suggests that women are likely cautious that the man could direct his aggression on her.

For a more concrete illustration: in high school, the athlete who is popular among high school girls is likely to dominate a player from their rival school. On game night, he is a "monster" on the football field. But becomes a completely different person on regular school days – likable, gentle, sweet.

Now let's see the difference between dominance and prestige.

Difference Between Dominance and Prestige

For humans, achieving social status and mating benefits are accomplished through compassion and cooperation, just as it is also achieved through aggression and intimidation. Experts and scholars believe that there are two ways to gaining social status – dominance and prestige.

Dominance

Dominance is brought about by coercion, threats, and intimidation. It is driven by *hubristic pride* – characterized by anti-social behaviors, conceit, arrogance, unstable relationships, high levels of disagreeableness and low levels of conscientiousness, poor mental health, narcissism, and neuroticism. Hubristic pride combined with arrogance and feelings of superiority enables dominance by encouraging behaviors of manipulation, aggression, and hostility.

Prestige

Prestige, on the other hand, is ushered in by a sense of accomplishment, success, and confidence. It is driven by *authentic pride* – characterized by rewarding interpersonal relationships, conscientiousness, agreeableness, positive mental health, and pro-social and achievement-oriented behaviors. Authentic pride is linked with "real" self-esteem, which is considering yourself as someone of value, rather than seeing yourself as superior to others.

Other people are inspired by individuals who exude confidence, those who are hardworking, agreeable, empathic, kind, energetic, nondogmatic, and those with "real" self-esteem.

These two routes have been observed in the *Tsimané* tribe, a tiny society in the Amazon. Here, dominance (was associated with physical size), while prestige was associated with generosity, the number of friends, and their hunting ability).

It is interesting to note that while proponents of acting dominant point to chimpanzees to prove the "exclusivity" of this route with the male status, new research revealed that even with primates, the alpha male status can be reached not just because one is strong and big, but also through the ability to be social and grooming others.

Adaptability and Flexibility

It might be tempting to conclude that based on the descriptions above, dominance is "negative" and prestige is "positive". What most people miss in discussions about being an alpha male or beta male is categorizing status should be based on *context*. A high-ranking officer of a Fortune 500 company is considered an alpha and is regarded to be part of the top tier in society. However, if the same man is put into the general population like a prison, he will find himself at the bottom of the hierarchy.

A man can be an alpha in a particular group, and become a beta in another.

In a challenging environment, the dominant male is always highly regarded since he can easily get anything, and he can give resources to anyone who will follow him. He only needs two important skills, these are intimidation and strength. But, beyond this purely vicious society, the prestigious male rules. He is built for success in any circumstance.

In a study conducted among university varsity athletes, the dominant students were found to be lacking in "real" self-esteem, agreeableness, and social acceptance, and more leaning towards aggression, disagreeableness, narcissism, and conscientiousness. These dominant males (as rated by their peers) are seen to possess higher leadership potential and athleticism, but lacking in cooperativeness, ethics, morality, helpfulness, and altruism.

Those who are considered to be prestigious individuals were found to be lacking in neuroticism and aggression, but has "real" self-esteem, agreeableness, social acceptance, and GPA. Also, prestigious individuals were ranked by their own peers and they were seen as more athletic and as better leaders. They are also deemed more intellectual, altruistic, helpful, ethical, moral, cooperative, and socially skilled.

The results showing dominance and prestige illustrate a variety to achieving status.

It is important to point out that one person can possess positive characters like leadership, strength, morality, and kindness. The two categories, *alpha,* and *beta* create a false dichotomy that clouds all the possibilities that a man can still achieve.

Dominance may be highly regarded and seen as beneficial in a limited set of circumstances, prestige is more valued in almost every context. With authentic pride, prestigious individuals tend to be more socially accepted, respected, and successful.

Another way of putting it: Dominance is seen as a short-term-term strategy to achieve success, and prestige is for the long-term. Dominance may allow you to conquer, but it is lacking in proper governance. Another dominant alpha male may inevitably come along and knock the "current" alpha male off his pedestal.

Bottomline

From the research presented, the ideal man to go out on a date with or become a romantic partner is someone confident, assertive, easygoing, and sensitive, without becoming demanding, dominant, aggressive, shy, or submissive. It is not about a man being alpha or beta. In other words, their ideal man is a prestigious man.

Chapter 3: The Laws of Manliness

Throughout history, we have studied and seen many strong men who became leaders of nations or armies. One of the most popular and regarded as one of the most notable examples of exuding "true manliness" was Theodore Roosevelt, the 26th President of the United States of America.

One of his influential quotes is:

"We need to iron qualities that go with true manhood. We need the positive virtues of resolution, of courage, of indomitable will, of power to do without shrinking the rough work that must always be done." – Theodore Roosevelt

There is a battle between masculinity and masculine values. Those who are weak, and are huge in terms of numbers, actually fear masculine values simply because they don't understand them and don't want to look and get sucked into the world of an imperfect society. Masculinity is what society "needs" more than ever. As society continues to stay defeated as it loses its strength as a community, people become more self-entitled, corruptible, less self-reliant, and more dependent on other people.

It is now time to bring back the "real men" and real and deserving leaders to bring back society's true strength.

Masculinity and strength are like cousins. Before men became heads of their own families, they were the leaders of their tribes, defending their tribes from beasts and evil men. They were both warriors and protectors. Men, to be called "men", should be strong, whether physically or spiritually. It is ideal if they are both physically and spiritually strong.

These men were champions and society and culture gained a lot from their boldness and clear purpose. They are never afraid. Never once did they flee or hide from challenges. It is their masculine values that should be brought back into popular culture.

These the Laws of Manliness. These were made for men not to simply confine every man into one single mode. They are free to become liberated, courageous, ambitious, and strong.

The Laws of Manliness

1. **Men should be self-reliant.**

   In today's society, self-reliance is starting to disappear among men. This is a society that is developing a certain sense of entitlement, where people feel that they deserve a few things without earning (just by praying or wishing for) them.

   Men should stop living on handouts from other people. Ask help if you need it, and accept it and then plan for how you are going to repay it.

   A man should learn to be self-reliant. It is acceptable to ask for support and guidance, but he should still be free to do what they think is best. Everything that he does, his life, his happiness, and his success all depend on him. Only someone weak would give away that power to someone else.

   Be the guy that offers support to others. Be a shoulder to cry on. Be there for them. You can worry about yourself later.

2. **To achieve success and happiness, you will have to work hard for it.**

Success is not something that lands on your lap easily. You are not born into it. Success is something that you need to work on.

Success in life is not just about having a successful career, the success we are talking about here is success in life in general.

Once you fail to recognize that success is all about hard work and not a birthright, and there is no other way to achieving it, you have lost. You have a weak resolve. You will try to fix things, that you may end up resorting to a quick fix rather than planning for long-term solutions. Failure might lead you to feel unhappy, unsatisfied, and poor. However, do not forget that failure is part of success. A man may experience failures before achieving long-term success.

3. **You have to create your own path. Enter the arena.**

This particular law is quite tricky. You might need to experience a lot of trial and error before finally achieving your goals. Expect to fail in life – and it will be a lot – but you have to go on and keep on fighting. These failures will help shape you as you figure out your own path, as you search out for the path that you want to take and the man you want to become.

But if you are too afraid to join the fight, you will never experience pain and eventual success. You have to step into the arena and learn how to fight your way. Be the guy who doesn't give up.

Follow your own path and set out to where others dare not go.

4. **Practice self-denial and forget about achieving instant gratification.**

We are living in a society that is full of instant gratification. This is a generation of credit card debts that are spent on items that we cannot really afford just to make an impression on others. We are so keen on impressing others, especially those people who don't like us.

But this attitude has to change. People have to change now!

If you look at some of the stories about great warriors and leaders in history, self-denial is common among them all. You can never get the job done without practicing self-denial.

Practice one day at a time. Identify the things in your life that may be hindering your growth, and eliminate them. Whatever they are, just get rid of them and change your routine. Replace these things with something that will help you move forward and continue fighting.

5. **When you fight for your values and principles, you will likely be standing alone.**

Don't be afraid if this happens. Remember that the weak will need the numbers simply because they have none.

It's cliché, but no one is an island – you will always need to have a strong support system. You need to have people who can teach you. You need leaders, teachers, and followers. Yes, you need them, but you don't need to have the numbers. There may be strength in numbers, but you don't need that because that strength already exists inside you.

Never crave the attention of others, nor seek their approval. Don't conform to what society is dictating – where your actions and your values are dependent on what others may think of you, and where you tend to change your thinking just so you will feel accepted.

It's the people who are not afraid to be true to themselves who become great leaders. Be that kind of leader.

Be you. Don't be a copycat. Be original.

Study some great men and you'll see that they were all unique in their way. They are original. Their actions were not dictated by what others may think of them.

6. **Continue fighting, even when you know you are going to lose, fight.**

You should never be afraid to get your hands dirty. Don't get intimidated by life itself – with all the challenges that go with it. People always remember people who continued despite having the odds not going their way. People remember warriors.

And when you decide to fight and fail, own up to the failure. Acknowledge that you failed. Do not blame your defeat on others. You should still be accountable for all your actions.

Most people may not have the courage to fight. When we say you fight, it doesn't mean that you shouldn't be cautious, because you should. However, if you need to protect something or someone, like your loved ones, your family's honor, or your friends, do not hesitate to stand up and protect them.

You should also do the same when it comes to your values – learn to fight for them – and don't back down just because they are not popular or not approved by the majority.

7. **Be accountable. Accept responsibility for your own actions and do not look for others to blame.**

    Honor seems to be something that is not highly regarded in modern society. People no longer feel responsible for their own words and actions. For most people, finding someone to blame is the easiest way out of any compromising situation. Instead of owning up to their mistakes, many individuals will always find someone to blame.

8. **Don't worry if you should fail, instead, worry if you don't even try.**

    A lot of people do not even try for fear of making a mistake and failing. They don't want to experience defeat, hence, they wouldn't even try. A coward fears just about everything and ends up doing nothing.

    Success is not achieved by shielding yourself from failures. Not trying at all is worse than failing.

9. **Be kind but don't let people take advantage of you.**

    You are not helping people by simply providing them what they need. This is a temporary solution – after some time when they have used up all of the "gifts" given to them, they'll be back begging for more.

    It's all right to give them at first, but you should also teach them to be self-reliant so that they don't have to beg for anything ever again. Invest your time to help them acquire the skills they need, rather than simply giving them money.

    Could money be enough? Sometimes, it is, yes. But only if they are given to the right people. There are those who, when given the opportunity, as a small amount of money, will think of ways on how to use it for their long-term benefit. They might find ways on how to invest the money or make a profit out of it.

    But, if given to the wrong person, they might end up becoming dependent, and simply wait for whatever would be given to them.

Money is also good when coursed through some charitable institutions that need them to build shelters, hospitals, and schools. By all means, give them money.

You can still be kind and help other people in any way that you can, but don't let them take advantage of you. Don't just give because you know it's the right thing to do.

You can be kind but don't be weak.

Do not attempt to carry other people all the time, instead, empower them.

10. Always be fair.

As society continues to evolve, a lot of manly qualities have been disappearing. The idea of fairness has been tainted. You might have already noticed that there are people who simply want to take what other people have worked hard for, without acquiring it on their own merit.

While it is good to help others because that's just how we are, and as humans, we have the responsibility to take care of the people who can't take care of themselves, but there should always be limitations to helping people.

It is good to look up to successful people and those who have accomplished a lot in life. But jealousy and envy are other things. It is not a good attitude to feel envious of the accomplishments of others, just because you have not achieved the same. Don't feel as if you were not given the same opportunities that successful people have received.

Don't say life isn't fair because others have had a good life and you didn't. This mentality is weak. Because you make the life you want.

It is not a matter of fairness. It is what you do with whatever is given to you.

A strong man will simply show respect and admiration for what another person has achieved in life. Rather than being envious, a strong man will want to accomplish what others have accomplished on his own accord. He will use the success of other people as inspiration to creating success for himself.

This is fair. This is just.

11. Never allow injustice.

Even in the olden days, men have always protected their tribes, their communities, their families. However, today, not all men protect their tribes. This modern world is full of evil people – cowardly men (and women) who take advantage of others who are weaker than them.

Some men molest and abuse weaker women and children. Some physically abuse their partners. Some kill for money and power.

The disappointing part is that society has turned a blind eye to injustice.

As a father, you have to protect your child. As a husband, you should protect your wife. As a son, you should protect your elderly parents. As a society, we should protect people who are vulnerable to attacks and vulnerable to being violated. As a society, we have a responsibility.

While some people would just turn a blind eye to the injustices they see, maybe for fear of their own life, you should never turn your back from people who might need you to protect and defend them.

12. Develop a habit of and a love for reading.

Read, you'll be surprised at the knowledge you can gain just by reading. Learn more about our heroes (if you haven't). Read to learn about other people's beliefs. Read to learn other people's opinions, particularly those that do not conform with yours. If you are a liberal, read up on something a conservative has written.

Be open.

Read up on religion, health, business, science, economics, and fitness. Learn about different cultures. Read up on the history of other countries. Read up on politics.

Reading is a way of traveling and learning without leaving your home. You'll find a lot of discoveries just by reading. Reading will open your eyes and your mind to the world. You'll learn that there is a whole lot of world out there.

13. Take time off weekly.

This is a fast-paced world we live in. People are always on the go. People are always trying to earn a living. Amid all the chaos in your everyday life, you need to disconnect even for just the weekend.

31

You have been working hard for the whole week, you should rest up, say, during the weekends.

Disconnect with the outside world and reconnect with yourself, even just once a week. It is easy to get overwhelmed with all the things that we need to handle in our day-to-day activities.

So, you need to stay still, relax, and enjoy the silence for a while. Disconnect. I mean, disconnect. Don't check your mobile phones, your tablet, your laptop, or computer.

Recharge. Relax. Enjoy the silence.

14. It's all right to laugh, especially at yourself.

We often hear people say that laughter is the best medicine. It is! It actually is!

Learn to enjoy life. Laugh more. Laugh at yourself. Make fun of yourself.

This is how you can cope with all the challenges you face every day. Learn to enjoy and appreciate the highs, and always find good in all the lows.

15. Don't be too dependent on the internet.

The internet is probably the most valuable innovation of this modern world. People use the internet to learn and search for information. It is a big platform wherein we can show the world who we really are. Social media is a huge thing. When walking down the street, you'll see people glued to their smartphones, tablets, or laptops.

People can now do business without leaving their offices, houses, or even their own countries. Families who are far away from one another can literally video call every day.

The internet simply bridged the gap.

But do not get caught up in this online world. Never let yourself be sucked into the virtual universe where some people create a different online persona.

Never give out personal information. Never give out too much about yourself on social media.

Today, you can find dates online. People talk online all the time.

Even young children have learned to use the internet.

While it is important to maintain an online presence, remember that this is not real life. You still have to live in the real world.

Don't get caught up with the online persona you are trying to project. You still have real friends that you can talk to face-to-face.

Social media is not tangible. Don't let yourself live in a space where "perfect" and "happy" people exist.

See the world. Enjoy the sunshine. Feel the wind on your skin. Smell the flowers.

The real world is where you should be.

16. Basic manners are always in style.

Even in our modern society where most people may not respond readily as they are supposed to, remember that the little things will go a long way. Basic manners will never go out of style.

Simple gestures like holding doors for others, pulling out chairs, saying thank you and please, or taking your hat off when you walk indoors, are still essential, not out of obligation, but out of respect for others. In this regard, when someone failed to thank you for holding the door for them, the best response is no reaction at all.

Practicing good manners is not a sign of weakness, in fact, it is a sign of the strength of character of the person giving it, a sign of respect for others, and an expression of love for the people you are with.

17. Treat people equally.

You should treat people as an equal. It doesn't matter if you are speaking with the chairman of a major company or the barista at your favorite coffee shop, or even your mother, you should treat them like they are the most important person present. Never look down on people that you see as inferior to you, nor should you put someone more popular on the pedestal.

18. Let your actions do the talking but be wise with your words.

Some people can talk for hours, while others don't (or can't or won't). Never brag about your wealth, or how powerful you are, or how successful you are. Let your actions do the talking. People will notice if you become successful. They will take notice if you become powerful.

They say that an empty tin can is loud, while a brand new can of food is not.

Just as you are accountable for your actions, you have to think before opening your mouth. Make sure you won't hurt someone when you reveal something. Consequently, you have to be firm with your actions for these will be your legacy to the world.

Think before you speak. Think before you act.

19. Remember that money isn't everything. Find life's real meaning.

Achieving your goals is good. Becoming successful in your career is good. Acquiring wealth is good. But don't let these things "own" you.

Success may be good but it is not everything. It is not the real meaning of life. Find your own meaning. Live for your family, loved ones, for your missions, and your faith. Don't live for your house, or your car, and other material things, instead, live for people. Live to find happiness.

Your fulfillment in life should not come from material possessions. Know what is really important.

Finding happiness, love, joy, peace, and helping others – these could be your life's meaning. Your life's meaning (or goals) should be attaining something spiritual within yourself.

20. Make the best of any situation you are subjected to.

There will be ups and downs in life. Welcome and enjoy the good things, but also accept the bad things.

Find the positive in everything. Find the lesson in every difficulty you face. Even those days that are filled with darkness and despair, always make the best of what is given. Never succumb to sorrows. Never blame others. Never try to run from them all.

Do not wish that you were someone else or that you were in another place.

Be a warrior! A real warrior will face challenges head-on.

Remember, be the best you can be. Maximize your full potential. Never accept mediocrity.

Go above and beyond.

Chapter 4: Characteristics of the Alpha Male

People refer to the alpha male as the "real man". How can you tell that a man is an alpha? What are the characteristics to watch out for? Do they have to possess special traits and characteristics? What makes women swoon over them?

Physical

- Voice

  For most women, the deeper the voice of a guy, the sexier he is. A man with a deep, full voice that exudes gravitas is seen as more manly, hence, more dominant. Heard the voice of actor, James Earl Jones? His voice is authoritative, and most people will always follow and listen to a man with that kind of voice quality.

Some studies prove that a man's voice can easily communicate dominance than spoken words. Surely, you won't get scared when a man threatens you with a cartoony voice, you might laugh at them, right? Now, if a man tells you to stay put with the voice of someone like Vin Diesel, you are likely to heed immediately.

It's probably a social status thing, but when a man has a bigger, deeper voice, they are perceived to be more of a leader, more dominant, and authoritative.

- Face

Good-looking men are likely to get a better first impression than men who are seen as less handsome. But having a handsome face doesn't easily make a guy socially dominating, it often depends on the kind of handsome.

Like, some men look ruggedly handsome, some are boyishly handsome (those they call baby face), and there are cute handsome men. The boy-next-door is not often seen as dominant, same with guys who are considered cute. When it comes to social dominance, ruggedly handsome men are more seen as strong, tough men, not to mention sexier. They are seen as more mature compared to men who are considered "cute".

- Eye contact

Men who are not intimidated to make eye contact when talking to other people are seen as more dominant. They are perceived to be always in control. For men who do not make eye contact are perceived to be shy, hence, unlikely to be seen as dominant.

- Physically fit

Men who are physically fit are likely to be seen as alpha males. They are perceived to be stronger.

- Body language and overall personality

You'll never catch a successful man slouching or walking slowly. They won't even go out of their house wearing wrinkled clothes.

Well-groomed men are easily seen as socially dominant. They look more trustworthy. It also helps if they convey strong and positive body language.

Other Characteristics and Notable Gestur1oes

- Confidence

This is probably the hallmark of alpha men. Confident men are easily seen as potential leaders.

- Touching

While there is a huge difference between the touch of a pervert and an alpha male. It's in the intensity of the touch and who is doing it. A pat on the shoulder is a sign of superiority and dominance.

- Competitive

Men who passionately compete are often perceived to be more desirable and successful than those men who just play the game just for the sake of playing. For the alpha male, competition is more serious. They are often picked as winners.

- Calm

A leader, an alpha male, will always keep their cool even during a difficult situation. They are less likely to be seen panicking. They always appear to be in control. Calmness even under pressure is seen as a good quality of a leader.

- No external validation

Alpha men don't need to seek the approval of other people. He doesn't doubt himself and his abilities. He already knows that he is a leader, at the top of the social hierarchy, he doesn't constant reassurance that is an alpha.

- Growth potential

Successful men believe in growth. For them, the only way to go is forward and upward. The alpha man doesn't hesitate to own up to his mistakes, instead, he takes each mistake as a learning experience to improve on himself. And he doesn't make the same mistake twice. He can easily give other people second chances.

- Problem solver

The alpha male does not sit around and mope whenever he is faced with a problem. He takes charge and seeks his team to solve any issue.

- Fearless

Alphas don't run away from problems. They face them all without hesitation. They are not afraid to make mistakes because they believe there are lessons to learn from every mistake you commit. They own up to their mistakes, they rectify the error, and then they move on.

- Ambitious and passionate

  Successful men are driven. They are passionate about work. They succeed because they are never afraid to strive hard in achieving their goals.

- Humble

  Despite their success, an alpha male remains humble. You won't see them brag about their accomplishments or the material things they own.

- High moral ground

  An alpha male sticks to his values and principles.

The alpha male does not consciously try to become an alpha male. This aspect is where most men fail. He is interested in life and lives his life like an adventure. He cares about other people. He works hard. He keeps himself physically fit. He takes every opportunity he is being given.

The alpha male goes out into the world without ever thinking they are alpha.

Now that's a true alpha male!

Chapter 5: Developing Your Physical and External Confidence

The alpha male exudes confidence. There are two forms of building confidence, internal and external. When we say internal confidence, it means that it is a state which is made up of what you think and how you feel about yourself. External confidence is based on the physical aspects, like the way you look, how much you weigh, how other people views sees you, and how much you are appreciated.

Fitness

What is your perception of yourself? Is it positive or negative? Studies show that there is a correlation between having self-confidence and physical and mental health. To be considered an alpha male, you have to have confidence. If you feel like you are lacking in this aspect, there are many different ways to make improvements. We start with your physical fitness.

There are five ways that exercise can improve your confidence, these are:

1. It makes you feel better.

   When you feel good physically, you'll also feel good mentally. Exercise helps you to break free from bad habits, like being sedentary, binge eating, and unhealthy eating habits.

   When you feel good, you are open to exploring new places, meeting new people, and you have the energy to overcome challenges.

2. It makes you feel stronger.

   Regular exercise strengthens your body. The risk of you developing high blood pressure and chronic disease is minimized. You get to control your weight easily.

   Exercise helps relieve stress, anxiety, and depression.

   Mentally and physically, you are stronger.

3. There is a sense of accomplishment.

   When you can create an exercise routine on your own and sticking to your chosen regimen it helps bring you a sense of accomplishment. When you successfully accomplish your exercise goals, you gain more emotional stamina to help you take on your personal goals, until you reach a point where you'll feel that there is nothing that you cannot do.

4. It helps boost your confidence.

   There are times when low self-confidence can be associated with body perception. Exercise regularly so that you can build your confidence by improving your body image. Exercise hits two birds with one stone – you become fit and you improve your confidence.

5. It increases brainpower.

   Aerobic exercises in particular feed the brain with essential vitamins and oxygen, thus improving your cognitive function. When you have a regular exercise routine, you become more focused, more alert, and it helps you complete the tasks at hand.

Boost Confidence with Proper Exercise

These are some of the physical activities that you can do that are proven to have the greatest effect on self-confidence.

- Aerobics

  Performing light aerobic exercise routines may help boost confidence. Keep a journal, write down how you felt before and after a routine. This helps you monitor emotional changes as you incorporate regular aerobics exercises into your day.

- Outdoor activities

  It may take only a few minutes to a maximum of 30 minutes to do some outdoor activities, like gardening, walking, running, or cycling. This helps improve your confidence, as well as your mood.

- Other physical activities that boost your mood:

  Yoga

  Weightlifting

  Strength training

  Tai chi

  Sports events in your community

  Volunteering (this will allow you to move around)

Find the physical activities that you enjoy and start being active. But make sure that you consult with your doctor before starting with any exercise routines.

Proper Diet

Researchers remain fascinated with the relationship between mental health and our eating habits. Achieving the right balance of nutrients from the food you eat can improve your mood and how you feel.

So, how do you eat your way to improving your confidence? Here's how:

- Food that helps boost your mood.

  Certain kinds of food are known to improve mood, these include:

  ✓ Carbohydrates – they are broken down into glucose that will supply the brain and muscles with energy. When you are consuming too little carbohydrates, you feel tired all the time and you can't concentrate. Unrefined carbohydrate food (fruits, vegetables, whole grains) helps sustain energy levels longer.

✓ Omega-3 Fatty Acids – studies show that omega-3 fatty acids help prevent depression because they directly affect most of the neurotransmitter pathways in your brain. Add oily fish to your diet, like salmon, sardines, trout, and mackerel.

✓ Vitamin D-rich food –is known to increase serotonin levels in the brain. You can get your supply of vitamin D from fortified cereals and oily fish

✓ Vitamin B-rich food –is essential in the production of energy. You can get vitamin B from broccoli, and spinach.

✓ Selenium-rich food – some studies prove that low levels of selenium result in a poor mood. You can get selenium from whole brazil nuts, grains, oats, beans/legumes, seeds, nuts, and seafood.

You should limit your consumption of the following:

▪ Sugar – a lot of people consume sweets if they are feeling low. It may work but only for a short while, however, eating sweets may cause fluctuations in your blood sugar levels, disrupting your mood completely. You will feel lethargic in the long run. You may replace sweet snacks with fruits or nuts.

▪ Caffeine – consuming too much coffee and caffeinated drinks may result in mild dehydration. It may also cause withdrawal headaches. Too much caffeine will disrupt your energy levels, resulting in mood swings, which after a while, might affect your confidence level. Reduce caffeine and instead drink more water or caffeine-free herbal teas.

▪ Alcohol – drinking alcohol may boost your confidence but only for a short time. Alcohol may act as both stimulant and depressant when drink too much. This will cause you to become irritable and anxious. Avoid drinking alcohol more than the recommended guidelines.

Personal Style

Most men are not concerned much with their personal style, especially if they are the manly type like the alpha male. Because of the natural charisma alphas have, they don't need to worry much about their style because they can look good in anything they wear.

However, looking good helps boost your confidence, and if your friends tell you that you need to change your style, you should heed.

Here are 10 helpful tips to boost your confidence:

1. The time is now!

    Whether it is losing weight, changing your eating habits, or moving – start now! Don't put your life on hold just because you haven't achieved all your goals. Invest in your overall look now. Believe me, you will feel much better about yourself, boosting your self-confidence, thus helping you achieve your goals.

    Look good, feel good. Feel good, do good!

2. Separate your issues about your body from your personal style.

    You don't need to have a well-toned body to have great style. Not all men are built the same, just as not all alphas have the "perfect" body and size. Don't let your imperfect body ruin your personal style. Instead, play up with your best features. Highlight them. Do you have broad shoulders? Choose shirts and suits that will highlight them.

3. You don't need clothes that make you feel bad about yourself.

    Get rid of the clothes that are too tight on you, or that you are not comfortable wearing. Most men do not like shopping for clothes, hence, they still have those shirts that they had when they were younger and slimmer. They still have in their closet those baggy jeans that were in style some years back. If you haven't used those shirts or pants for the last year, pack them away, or you may give them out to charity.

4. Self-appraisal may do you good.

    Think about the items in your closet that make you happy or that you feel good wearing. You might have that shirt that people compliment you on when you're wearing them. Or you have a suit that makes you feel confident whenever you wear it to the office.

Learn to compliment yourself for looking good. Take a mental note of how you feel when you wear a particular shirt or suit. Hold on to that feeling and try to replicate that feeling when you are wearing other shirts.

Remember to wear clothes that make you feel good about yourself.

5. Don't be embarrassed when others compliment you.

Men do not usually feel comfortable when people notice how good they look. Just the same, some men worry about what other people will think about the clothes they wear.

When people compliment you, take it and thank them, plain and simple. Take it as a win, and feel confident. Own it.

One way of being comfortable about getting compliments is to give compliments to other people. If you notice a colleague looking good in their clothes, tell them they look great. You'll be surprised at how good you'll make them feel.

6. Step out of your comfort zone.

It will not be easy stepping out of your comfort zone. Don't rush. Take it slowly. If you need to change your looks completely, do it gradually and do things with subtlety. If you decide to wear shirts that are not in your usual color palette, don't go out wearing them from head to toe. For instance, you don't fancy brightly colored shirts, but you'd like to try them, wear them with your favorite jeans.

See how this particular fashion style makes you feel. Are you comfortable wearing it? When you feel comfortable and you feel good about yourself when wearing that, then consider that it's the right color for you.

7. Take inspiration from other men who have good styles.

When you take inspiration from others, make sure that you don't simply copy them. Your choice of style should be all about you – personality, figure, height, skin color, and your lifestyle. Develop your own style while you take inspiration from others. Choose someone who is a known male fashion icon or it could be someone you know, like a friend.

8. Begin with good foundations.

Right-fitting underwear will give you so much confidence because it helps you feel good.

9. Act confidently, even if you're not.

You'll often hear from people *"fake it 'til you make it"*. The more you appear confident, the more it becomes real. Don't think about wearing the "right" shirt when going to the office, or when you have to run an errand. Don't think about being overdressed. People will always have an opinion about what you are wearing, simply get over it and don't overthink.

Exude confidence when you step out with a new sleek suit. Feel good about it. Be confident with it.

10. Get yourself as a personal stylist.

If you feel like what you have been doing is not working, maybe you need to hire a personal stylist. Yes, it is a thing. They will assess you and choose clothes that will fit your lifestyle, personality, and personal preferences. They will be able to help you be comfortable in the style that you choose.

These tips are not rocket science, it is easy to begin implementing them.

Grooming

Having confidence is just as important as intelligence or skills in getting ahead in life. When you are confident, you can easily project an image that everyone will want to be a part of.

Being confident is projecting an appealing image. Even if you are wearing the most flattering suit to a meeting with investors, if you have poor grooming, you'll never close a deal. Men are not too particular about their grooming habits, unlike women, but there are few things to remember in terms of improving your grooming habits.

- If you go for beard keep it neat and clean

- If you go for shaving do it Regularly

While you may have been shaving regularly for many years, there is still a lot to learn. The technique is important rather than the tools you use.

A practical tip: after applying shaving cream, let it sit on your face for about one to two minutes before you begin shaving. This technique "softens" your face for an easy shave.

- Trim those nose hairs.

  For a lot of people, visible nose hairs are disgusting. Did you know that a single noise can distract other people's attention? It also creates a bad impression about your habit, that you have poor grooming.

  You only need a trimmer (or scissors) with a round tip. Ideally, remove nose hairs every few weeks.

- Haircuts

  Grooming experts agree that a well-groomed and confident alpha male should never make it appear that they recently got a haircut. The rule of thumb is, you should maintain a consistent look so that other people will always have the same, positive perception of you.

  It is also not advisable to use hair products. Always maintain that natural look.

  Consequently, if you often get comments like *"You look like you need a haircut",* then you better get one more often. A haircut at three weeks interval would be ideal.

Chapter 6: Acting and Communicating Confidently

How you interact with other people – through actions and other communication platforms – is important. How you act while having a conversation with others is more important compared to your spoken words. Exuding confidence in front of other people doesn't necessarily mean you can always get what you want.

Your actions and your communicating techniques are influenced by a lot of factors, including, your overall attitude, your body language, your verbal communication, acting with confidence like a true gentleman, and handling of criticisms from other people.

This chapter discusses all these.

Attitude

When you are confident about yourself and you have a positive attitude, you have the power to take control of your life and the behavior of other people. No matter what happens, you are an alpha male, and you are the only one in charge.

What exactly is attitude? It is the way you think and the way you act – your attitude says a lot about you.

Attitude is an important part of confident communication.

People can *see* your attitude in the way you act. They can *hear* your attitude in the tone of your voice. Attitude is an *expression* in itself. It is powerful. It can serve as a mirror into the deepest of your thoughts.

A positive attitude always brings positive results. The same goes with a negative attitude bringing negative results.

When communicating with other people, it is better to have the right attitude rather than to struggle to make the other person understand your point. With the right attitude, you avoid becoming impatient if others fail to understand your concerns.

With the right attitude, you don't need to compete or struggle to achieve a particular outcome.

Have the Right Attitude for a Better and More Positive Communication

- Avoid using negative words – This may be the simplest thing to do but it is the most difficult to achieve. But with practice, it can be done. Try not to use negative words like *unable to, won't, will not, cannot*, etc. Rephrase sentences to avoid using negative words, but making sure it still has the same meaning. For instance, rather than saying, *"This just cannot be done if you can't provide your specific requirements"*, say *"If you can give us your specific requirements, we can complete the project on time"*.

- Always look at the bright side of things – Disappointments, missteps, and challenges will happen, but you should always see the positive aspect you can get out of this negativity.

- Come up with other options and solutions – For some reasons, there will be things that cannot be possibly done. Rather than create further disagreement, study the situation and come up with other possible options. Outright rejection of a proposal could be the easier route, but doing so won't solve the problem. Coming up with alternative solutions indicates that you are someone who is willing to go the extra mile in order to get things done.

- Never force, never coerce – When you are asking another person to perform a task or when you are refusing to perform a task, be as polite as possible. Avoid using *should* or *should not, you must* or *you must not* because they are plain forceful and impolite. Not one person wants to be forced to do anything, would you? Instead, use positive phrases like *can we* or *let's just do this,* etc.

- Sound helpful – Use a voice that ensures the other person that you are willing to help. No matter how negative a situation is, tell the other person that you are ready to help. This doesn't just give assurance to the other person, but it also makes you a helpful person.

A positive attitude goes a long way and it gives you the confidence you need to become an alpha male.

Body Language

Body language affects other people's perception of you, hence it is important to learn how to use your body language to your advantage.

To improve your confidence with the use of your body language, these are what you can do:

- Proper posture is important – You'll have to maintain an assertive posture. To project confidence, your legs should be aligned with your shoulders, while your feet should be about four to six inches apart. Keep your shoulders back and turn your body towards the other person. When you are standing, slightly push your head up to the sky. This is your assertive position.

  An assertive posture projects confidence. It shows that you are not insecure and you are open to the other person you are talking with.

  Avoid the submissive position – hands folded in front, legs crossed, or weight is pressed down on one hip. A more confident posture, when standing upright, your feet should be firmly on the ground.

When you are sitting, your back should be straight, your rear should be towards the back of the chair. Your feet should be planted firmly on the floor.

- Create your own power poses – According to experts, just two minutes of the different power poses can help you feel and look confident. These involve "open" body poses that will take up space. It will tell the brain that you are feeling confident, in turn, the brain will produce more testosterone while lowering levels of cortisol (stress hormone).

A lot of men suffer from low self-confidence and feelings of powerlessness because of their social status, their "rank" in society, or their lack the resources.

- Watch the gestures that you do with your hands – One of the most important parts of body language is hand gestures. You don't want to find yourself poking a finger in someone's face, that would be an aggressive gesture. When trying to make a point, you may simply have an open palm while keeping your fingers together.

An open hand with the palm facing upwards is a positive gesture which means openness, trustworthiness, cooperation, and acceptance. On the other hand, your hands on your hips connote arrogance or impatience. Crossing your arms may mean being closed off and defensive.

When in front of a crowd or group, avoid making negative hand gestures. Clicking your pen, or tapping your nails on the table, or playing with your hair are signs of nervousness and lack of confidence.

- Be mindful of your face – You should have a "standard face" – the fact that other people see when you are looking at them or listening to them, or when you are not saying a thing. Alpha males are expected to have a stern face. When you have a strong "standard face", people might avoid talking to you because you may appear unapproachable to them.

You can still appear confident and authoritative without making a strong facial expression. Try to relax your face and smile more often, while keeping your face firm.

- Maintain eye contact – Proper eye contact when talking with other people means you are sincere, honest, confident, and approachable. Avoiding eye contact may mean insincerity or dishonesty. It also projects submissiveness. Proper eye contact is not aggressive that you make others uncomfortable.

- Mirror the other person's body language – To build rapport, try mirroring another person's body language. Sit the way the other person is sitting. You may also mirror their expressions, hand movements, or mannerisms. But be careful so as not to appear as mimicking them, because you might come off as inappropriate. Make it appear as natural as possible.

- Avoid fidgeting – This is a sign of lacking confidence and nervousness. Fidgeting might also distract other people from wanting to get to know you. Be mindful of what triggers your fidgeting habits, try to replace those habits.

Looking confident with the use of your body language is easy. The key is not to let your body language undermine what you want to do as a leader, as an alpha male.

Verbal Communication

In most situations, it's useful to communicate with assertiveness and confidence. To become an alpha male, you'll have to learn to present yourself with confidence.

When you are talking with other people, you are communicating via two channels at the same time – verbal and nonverbal channels. To be able to send a clear message, you'll have to make sure that the message is consistent enough through these two communication channels. Hence, if you use positive, confident words, in the hopes of portraying a confident self-image, it is equally important that your nonverbal communication cues project the same level of positivity and confidence.

The use of an intelligent script of words will make you look confident and knowledgeable, it will have a different impact on your audience if your nonverbal cues support or contradict those words.

Your goal should be to be perceived as assertive and confident, not as someone aggressive or overbearing. But it will still depend on how the other person interprets your words and your actions. For one person, you will achieve your goal of being seen as assertive and confident, but another would see you as overly aggressive. It's all about context.

Tips on How to Improve Your Verbal Communication Skills

To be seen as confident, to be able to command respect, and to help you build rapport with others, you should be able to speak confidently, clearly, concise, and with poise. A man is perceived to be an alpha male if he can do all that.

- Learn to organize your thoughts.

  It is wise to think before you speak. You'll convey your message better if you can eliminate a lot of awkward pauses that may come when you begin speaking. This is why you must organize your thoughts even before you open your mouth. It is always more effective if you keep it short and concise, plus, it will create more impact, rather than spinning your words that can lead to becoming pointless. When you're responding to a question or trying to give your opinion on some matters, take a minute to think about what you are going to say.

- Make it short, clear, and impactful.

  As mentioned earlier, you can easily get your point across if you keep it clear and concise. Don't try using too many complex sentences to come off as smart and knowledgeable. Remember, the simplest of words are the easiest to understand.

  So, while gathering your thoughts, ask yourself, *"What could be the best way to make my point, that they can easily understand?"*

- Talk with confidence.

  When you come off as confident and sure of yourself, people will see you as someone they can trust and respect. These can impact your ability to confidently speak:

  > *command of the topic/subject matter,*
  > *choice of words,*
  > *the tone of your voice,*
  > *body language, and*
  > *ability to make eye contact.*

- Vocal tone is important.

  No matter how eloquent you'll speak or how great your ideas are, if you speak in a monotone voice, people will lose interest. To emphasize important points, use voice inflection and change the pitch of your voice as you speak (to show emotion). Doing so will sustain the interest of your audience.

- Actively listen.

It's not enough to be a good speaker, being a good listener is just as important. This will also improve your verbal interactions with the people around you because you'll be able to respond accurately. These are the five stages of active listening:

1. *Receiving*

2. *Understanding*

3. *Remembering*

4. *Evaluating*

5. *Responding*

When you actively listen, it sends a message to the people you are talking to that you genuinely care about their opinions and ideas. It lets them know that you understand their needs. It is also better if you can summarize what you've heard or ask clarifying questions.

You will gain their trust and you'll be able to build rapport.

- Be mindful of nonverbal communication cues.

Remember that your body language has an impact on how people will interpret your attitude and your spoken words. Make sure that you are aware of your gestures, your changing facial expressions, and the rest of your body language so that they are aligned with what you are trying to say.

Likewise, you must be able to read the body language of the people in front of you. Make eye contact while talking to them so you'll be able to see their doubts or lack of interest.

- Consider your audience's perspective.

Just because you know the subject matter quite well doesn't mean that your audience has the same knowledge as you. Take into consideration how they will be able to understand the message you are trying to relay. This is particularly true if they don't have the technical knowledge about the topic. So, don't try to impress them by using complex words, simplifying them is key.

Acting Like a Gentleman

The meaning of being a gentleman has changed throughout the years. Historically speaking, the title gentleman was a birthright. Those men who were born to wealthy families and with good social standing were considered gentlemen. During this time, these men simply inherited the title through their family.

Over time, its meaning has changed and evolved. The term gentleman was no longer associated with men born into nobility.

The title included men who worked to achieve their prominent social status. The word gentleman evolved into a term to politely describe a *man of character*.

What does it mean to be a gentleman in the modern world?

Today, to be considered a gentleman is based on a man's honor, morality, and values. Gentlemen hold themselves to a high set of standards of conduct. Considerate, calm, and polite are the cornerstone to which a gentleman is defined.

A gentleman is seen as a chivalrous man towards women. This means that they treat women with respect and with utmost courtesy. They are attentive to what a woman needs and wants, but they also know their own value and purpose.

When a gentleman asks a woman for a date, he will be the one to choose the place and time. He will take into consideration the woman's likes and interests. He will let the woman walk in front of him, as he protects her from behind, especially when walking through a dark walkway.

Being a gentleman is more than just giving his woman flowers, or pulling the chair for her, or opening doors for her. We can say that these are just *small acts of noble kindness*.

A gentleman is someone who is sure of himself, certain of what he wants to say and how he acts, and he will do so with confidence. Qualities also describe an alpha male.

How to Act Like a Gentleman: While Speaking

You may be the perfect alpha male – charming and good looking – but to be a true gentleman, you have to remember these:

- Don't speak like someone you're not.

Don't talk like an Englishman when you're not, just because you want to sound cool. Men and women alike find the British accent sexy, but that doesn't mean you have to pretend like you are one. Stick to your natural way of speaking and tone of voice.

- Listen to what others have to say.

  It is easy to become self-centered in this modern society. Do you always find yourself preferring to hear only yourself as opposed to other people? The perfect gentleman doesn't interrupt others while they are speaking, just as you wouldn't want other people to interrupt when you're talking. It's a simple way to show respect. Listening also allows you to respond or react accordingly.

- Mind your manners.

  Never underestimate the importance of saying *thank you* and *please*.

- Resist the urge to talk about yourself all the time.

  Nobody has ever liked an individual who constantly talks about himself. This is almost as important as listening to the other person. When somebody simply asks you how you've been, don't go on talking lengthily about everything that is happening to you.

- Avoid swearing all the time.

  An occasional slip of the tongue is forgivable, but don't make it a habit to cuss most of the time. It connotes negativity and a lack of respectability.

How to Act Like a Gentleman: In Public

Public places include the grocery store, restaurant, gym, coffee shop, or post office.

- Open the door for anyone.

  This applies to everyone, male or female, alpha or not. It is polite to hold the door for the person following you as you enter the door.

- Be courteous to store staff, the cleaning lady, or the waiter. No matter what the social status of an individual is, whether they are above you or below you, treat them equally and with respect. Never demand special treatment just because you work in a big company.

- Dress appropriately.

  Surely, you won't get caught wearing your pajamas to the office, right? A gentleman always looks respectable wherever they are. It doesn't mean that you have to wear suits all the time, a clean and simple white shirt would suffice.
- Avoid being loud or disruptive.

  A gentleman doesn't make a scene in public places where he becomes vulnerable. For once, such crude behavior.

How to Act Like a Gentleman: While Driving

- Stop at pedestrian crossings.

  It doesn't matter if there are people waiting to cross, or how slow or how fast they walk, you should always allow pedestrians to cross.
- Do not drive your car behind someone's vehicle.

  Driving so close to the back bumper of another car may be indicative of your impatience. This is plain rude and impolite.
- Do not honk unless you are in imminent danger.

  Unless there is a vehicle behind you that's about to collide with your car, there is no particular reason to honk your car horn. It is impolite and a sign of disrespect.
- Do not rev up your engine.

  Similar to honking your horn, revving up your car's engine is nothing more than letting people know that you know how to press a pedal down. Plus, it's a total waste of money. Unless you are in a racing event, it is impolite and immature.

How to Act Like a Gentleman: If You're a Guest

Whether you're attending a dinner party or simply staying with a family member, it is still important to act like a guest. Here's how:

- Call ahead.

  Calling your host prior to your arrival is a polite gesture. It allows them to prepare. Never show up unannounced. If you are running late, it is just as important to inform your host.

- Bring a little gift.

  Your gift depends on the occasion or situation. Just think about what the host may have a use for. If you are not sure what to bring, you may call your host and ask what you can bring.

- Send a *thank you* note.

  Show your appreciation by sending a *thank you* note to your host, one to two days after your visit.

How to Act Like a Gentleman: When You're in a Relationship

- Remember the little things.

  Make it a point to remember the little things that another person values. Like, if there's a particular candy that she likes, buy her some. Your significant other will appreciate it.

- Open the car door for her.

  Modern men do not do this anymore. Be different, be a gentleman and an alpha male.

- Never expect things to be done.

  Do not expect your partner to make dinner for you. Do not expect her to wash your clothes. When a man starts expecting women to do things like these, she begins to feel unappreciated. Take it upon yourself to do them every now and then.

- Pride does not belong in any relationship.

  When you are having an argument, be willing to listen to her side of the story. If you did something wrong, admit it and apologize.

These are just sample scenarios. The main point is, being a gentleman means being sure of yourself, having confidence, and never failing to be polite. Take it upon yourself to improve and be a better alpha male.

Handling Criticism

Being able to graciously handle criticisms is a class act. Dealing with it positively is an important life skill. There will be instances when you'll be criticized. Sometimes it would be difficult to process, but everything actually depends on your reaction.

You have a choice to either take it positively to improve or negatively that can cause stress, anger, and loss of self-confidence.

When we are challenged by another person, it is natural that we react negatively. But this shouldn't be an excuse because you have the power to change it.

Constructive or Destructive Criticism

When a colleague becomes critical of your work, you get hurt and it may cause you to doubt yourself. Destructive criticisms are often made with malicious intent. But it can also mean that the other person was just being thoughtless.

On the other hand, constructive criticism points out your mistakes and gives alternative solutions on how to resolve a misstep. It helps you to make improvements.

How to Deal with Critical People

- Keep in mind that people who criticize are plain envious of your success.

- Never respond in anger and do not create a scene in public.

- Remain calm and continue to understand and respect the other person.

- If you feel you are going to burst into anger, immediately walk away. Never engage right there and there.

How to Turn it Around

- It is human nature to make mistakes. No matter what kind of criticism being hurled at you, analyze it and find the lesson. Make it a learning experience.

- Don't take criticisms personally.

- Do not take them lightly. Use these criticisms to improve yourself.

Everybody learns from mistakes. Learning from every mistake is the perfect way to learn.

Chapter 7: Living Confidently

Every one of us will have moments in our lives when we feel insecure, but a lack of confidence is actually a burden. Self-doubt will prevent you from living your life to the fullest.

You can overcome self-doubt.

Happiness

For most people, happiness is elusive. Many people search for happiness, but always end up "empty-handed". Happiness is not something that someone can give you. it is a state of mind, created from within you.

Here are the "keys" to happiness:

- Keep a journal where you can write down your milestones, breakthroughs, and achievements. Every time you are doubting yourself, go back to that list and see how far you've come.

- Enjoy the little things. These are often not appreciated. Even if you bought a pen in your favorite color or a fancy cup you recently bought, appreciate and enjoy them.

- Do what you love. Never settle. If you haven't found it yet, keep on looking, and soon you'll find it.

- Create a perfect day. You have the power to change your perspective, thus completely changing the way you live.

- Positive affirmations are effective. Repeatedly tell yourself that today is going to be good, and wait for it because it will be a good day. Happiness begins when you learn to alter your mindset. Eliminate the negative thoughts and replace them with positive affirmations.

- Accept that you're not perfect. No one is. We live in a rather imperfect world. Do not compare yourself to others. Appreciate yourself, accept yourself.

- Surround yourself with happy, positive people. Friends and family can always bring out the best in you.

Keep on going, you might stumble and fall, but you just have to keep moving forward.

Being Likable

For alpha males, the more they become confident, the less likable they become. People like the underdogs – those who are humble.

How do you balance confidence and humility then? Having confidence is a feeling that we all experience. How we let others "see" this feeling will be the determining factor if others will see us as confident or egotistical.

- Shift your attention to how you can make others feel better about themselves when they are with you. This makes you appear less egotistical.

- Acknowledge your strengths and never apologize for them. Recognize your weaknesses and see how you can improve. Likewise, acknowledge the strengths of other people.

- Keep in mind that there is always someone better than you at something.

- Think twice whenever you feel the need to prove yourself.

Trust and Respect

Trust and respect are hard to earn and easily lost. These are two of the most important characteristics of being a good leader. Workers look up to their superiors for guidance. The trust of the workforce in their superiors has a huge impact on their productivity.

So, as an alpha male, what does it take to earn the trust and respect of the people under you?

- Free and open communication. This is important in building trust and respect. Open door policies have many facets. Create an environment where people will feel safe to come to you when they have concerns, new ideas, or constructive criticisms.

- Be consistent. This is how your people will trust you.

- Don't be afraid to get your hands dirty. Letting your people feel that you will not hesitate to roll up your sleeves and do the dirty work may earn the trust and respect

- Be firm and stand by your decisions, these are the marks of a real alpha male. You have to be confident with whatever you decide. There shouldn't be any dilly-dallying.

- Be generous in sharing your knowledge. Great leaders create more leaders, not followers.

Handling Self-Doubt

In an instant, self-doubt can ruin everything for you. Here are tips on how to handle self-doubt:

- Don't make excuses. It is human nature to be afraid to fail so when we do, we find excuses, we look for people and circumstances to blame. Rather than owning to the mistakes, people find it easier to put the blame on someone or something.

- Be aware of the closed circle that you keep. On average, there are at least five people that we spend most of our time with. These people have an effect on us. When you spend time with them, do you ever feel doubt about yourself or you become more confident? After talking to them, do you leave feeling better or you only became worse? These are questions to ask yourself if you want to stick with these people who might be influencing you to doubt yourself.

- Increase self-awareness. This is a powerful personal development tool. Go to the underlying causes of your self-doubt. What triggers it? Is it because of your lack of knowledge in some areas? Resolve by studying. Could it be a fear of talking in front of a crowd? You can overcome this by practicing and making sure you have all the information you need before speaking.

- Don't be hard on yourself. Counter self-criticism with self-compassion. It is simply being kind to yourself.

- Never ask for validation from others. Seeking advice from other people is beneficial, but if it becomes a habit of soliciting advice before making important decisions, it is not healthy. Believe in your ability to find solutions to current issues.

- Stop talking about your plans. Studies are proving that when you keep on telling others about your goal and they acknowledge it, you may not do the work needed to achieve that goal. The reason is that the brain will assume the *talking for the doing*. The instant gratification you get from other people acknowledging your goal tricks your brain into feeling that it has already been achieved.

- Trust in your values. It is easier to come up with decisions when they are aligned with your values.

- Start acting. Don't allow self-doubt to cripple you into not trying. Go with your gut and start now.

Career

Some people lack confidence in themselves and their abilities. Take note that these are usually well-educated and talented people. Then at some point in their lives, they allow negative situations to foster self-doubt.

Once you let a limiting belief take over, it will change your outlook in life. You begin to look for validation that you are not smart enough, and you will always find something that affirms that belief. For example, in a meeting, a colleague gives a different opinion from yours. Rather than acknowledge or be open to discussions, you keep quiet or you become defensive. You end up beating yourself up for not being smart enough because you didn't think about it first.

Confidence is integral in becoming successful in the career you choose. Confidence is essentially knowing what you are good at.

If you are confident you become more assertive so people will begin to take you seriously. You can do more if you are confident about your abilities. When you're confident, you communicate with others more effectively.

Effective communication is essential for career advancement.

Chapter 8: Alpha Traits You Should Develop

Every man wants to become an alpha. Most guys want to be the guy who other men will respect and women to get attracted to. If you want to become a true alpha male, here are the top traits you need to develop.

Courageous

An alpha doesn't fear anything. He doesn't let fear take over. An alpha fights through this fear. He may feel anxious to start a new business, but he will push through with it.

Easily Controls His Emotions

When faced with challenges, the alpha male does not succumb to pressure, instead, he will take a few deep breaths, then he will evaluate the situation to come up with the next best action. He will not lash out emotionally.

Has a Purpose

He knows what his purpose in life is. He knows where to go and what to do. He doesn't just float around endlessly.

He Makes the Decisions and Stands by Them

Most people fear making decisions because they are afraid that something might go wrong with the decisions they made. A real alpha male is a born leader and they are good decision-makers.

He is Not Afraid to Speak His Mind

In this modern world, people have become too sensitive. And a lot of them prefer not to speak about their thoughts for fear of rejection.

The alpha male is different. He doesn't back down when he needs to tell the truth. While there is a little fear, he pushes that fear aside and states his honest opinions on issues.

He is Not "Governed" by Rules

Alphas recognize that there should be a balance in life. He doesn't let his career ruin his relationships. He knows that work, health, love, family, and friends are important aspects of his that need to be cultivated to remain strong.

He Keeps Himself Fit

Feeling good starts from within. A strong and healthy body helps the mind to be strong and healthy, too.

You have to learn to value your health because if you are not healthy, you cannot work on achieving your goals. Keep yourself fit. Exercise. Eat a balanced diet.

Alphas are Not Afraid to Say "No"

It is inevitable for people to come to you for favors. An alpha male will not blindly give in to the whims of other people. He is not a pushover. He can confidently say "no", but still with kindness. He doesn't do it out of contempt, but because he is just looking out for his best interests.

He is Aware of His Weaknesses and Recognizes Them

Most egotistical men do not acknowledge their weaknesses, because they'd rather focus on their strengths. fair enough, though. But ignoring your weaknesses will not be a good idea.

The alpha male does not worry about his weaknesses. He doesn't even deny having these weaknesses. He recognizes these his weaknesses and finds ways ho to fix them.

He has Good Posture

This last item is a physical one. You'll never catch alphas slouching or staring down at their feet when talking to people. He has a strong and confident posture.

70

Chapter 9: The Passionate Alpha

Alpha males are passionate people. Passion is the love for whatever you are doing. It's all about what you want in life. It is your core being.

Passionate living needs a sense of authenticity. You can't be passionate about something if you do not really believe in it.

What are the characteristics of a passionate alpha male?

Keep on reading:

- Early birds – The passionate male tend to start their day earlier than most people, especially if they are scheduled to do something they are passionate about that day. They are just too excited to take action.

- Consumed by passion – A passionate alpha male's thoughts and actions tend to circle back towards the things they are passionate about.

- They feel more than just the usual excitement – Once people find their passion, they feel intensely for it. For example, one who is passionate about books will have an extension collection of books, some of which they haven't read first. An avid runner would join more than one marathons a year.

- They feel more than the typical disappointment – Because they feel more than the usual excitement whenever they pursue their passion, their disappointment is equally "huge". Often, the people around them do not understand why the passionate male is devastated whenever he can't do the thing they are passionate about. Other people would never understand unless they find something to be passionate about.

- Passionate males are high rollers – They are risk-takers. They believe so much in the things they are doing or the cause they chose to support that they are willing to take risks that most people won't even try taking.

- Their passion gets their unmatched devotion – There are a lot of things that we need to focus on in our lives. But for passionate males, they tend to focus their time and effort on something that they think is worthy. They have mastered the art of excellent time management to attend to every aspect of their lives. A perfect example of this is professional bodybuilders. They put their effort, time, and dedication to pursue that passion. They follow a strict menu plan to build strong and toned muscles.

- Completely immersed in their passion – When one is committed to their work (or anything they are passionate about), they tend to bring them home. That's how dedicated they can be. Their lives essentially revolve around what they are passionate about, whether that's their family, charity work, advocacy, sport, or a hobby. One thing is certain, almost every aspect of their lives revolve around their passion.

- They cannot stop talking about their passion – Maybe because they are too excited about their passion that they can't help themselves. Sometimes, the people around them have had enough of hearing their stories over and over again. They are just overflowing with so much passion, excitement, and pride.

- For them, they are all-in – When they are passionate about something, they don't have reservations. Either they will go full speed or not at all. That's how they love the things they are passionate about. They don't care if they crash and burn. Though, this doesn't happen all the time. Most passionate people, do achieve their goals. For some, it was just a lack of experience and knowledge that they fail. For those people who have been doing this for a long time, they have learned how to manage their time and resources so their productivity doesn't suffer.

- They look forward to a bright future – They look at their future and know that it will be bright and full of potential. Hence, they are willing to risk everything just to pursue their passion.

Chapter 10: Alpha Male – Charisma

The alpha male has a certain charm in them. They are a magnet not just for women. While some alphas are naturally charismatic, it is a quality that you can learn and master. Charisma has nothing to do with how you look, or your race, or your personality.

Though charisma is not something that we can physically see, its effects manifest to the people who encounter them. People around the charismatic person will feel it and naturally react positively.

The whole room seems to light up in the presence of charismatic men. People are naturally drawn to a charismatic man – they would watch him, they would listen when he starts to talk, and they get involved in anything that he takes interest in.

You can be one too!

We are not born with charisma but we all have that natural vibe to be charismatic. And it can be enhanced by improving confidence and social skills.

Being true to who you are is good, then you add in some skills and socializing techniques and you will develop charisma in no time.

What Makes an Alpha Male Charismatic?

- He has the ability to feel strong emotions.

   Most men hide their emotions, they feel uncomfortable showing their true emotions, so they remain safe and polite. People will get bored with you when you don't show real emotions.

   Charismatic men are different. They are socially intelligent enough to show emotions and the people around will feel them.

- He can easily compel other people to feel the same emotions as he does.

   An alpha man who has an infectious personality can encourage others to "copy" his body language and adopt the emotion and attitude he feels at that moment. And he isn't even aware he has that effect simply by just showing his real emotion and interest in the subject matter he is discussing.

- He is his own man.

   A huge part of being a charismatic alpha man is possessing excellent social skills and a complete understanding of people. A confident man doesn't worry about what other people think of him. He doesn't concern himself about other's opinions about him. He doesn't doubt himself and he does not compare himself with other men.

   When a man doesn't have insecurities, it resonates in his whole being. He is confident about himself and his abilities. No other people can make them doubt themselves.

How Charismatic Men Act in Social Situations

Most charismatic men actually don't have an answer to the question of why people, especially women, are easily drawn to them. But the best way to find out is to observe a charismatic man when in the presence of other people. Look for how they use their body language, watch out for their communication style, and observe how they handle social interactions with others, particularly with women.

One thing that would be noticeable in charismatic men is that they do not even try too hard to gain the attention of other people. You won't see them try hard to be the center of attention in a group. They would rarely speak about themselves.

People are just naturally drawn to them because they are real and genuinely likable.

Golden Rule of Charisma

Why do most alpha males exude charisma? Because they make other people feel good about themselves, rather than focusing on making themselves feel good (because of the attention they might be getting).

If you want to be charismatic, stop making it about you and start focusing on other people and how they may feel when they are around you.

However, it doesn't mean that you have to become Mr. Complimentary all of a sudden. Your compliments have to be real, if you overdo them, you will appear to be insincere and your compliments unreal.

Keep it real! Always!

Chapter 11: Alpha Male – Leadership, Lead by Example

To be considered a true leader, you should be able to influence a community or a group of people to achieve goals and objectives. A leader is someone people follow.

In today's modern society, leaders are not born, they are instead raised or they are groomed to lead. Becoming a leader is a process. Some people are comfortable and confident enough to lead, while others shy away from it.

The alpha male is considered a leader.

Many of them are natural leaders – in time they developed certain skills a leader should acquire, hence, they become the right fit to lead their social circles.

Leadership is a skill that any man can acquire and develop. With the right timing, resilience, and proper knowledge, you can develop important leadership skills, just like learning how to ride a bike or learning how to cook.

If you are a leader, there are two ways with which people will follow you, these are *power* and *influence*.

The definition of power is your ability to enforce your will on other people to make things happen by requiring your subordinates to abide by your commandso. Some people use the power given to them wisely, some don't. Possessing power can be tricky and you should use it sparingly, on a per need basis because it can be open to potential abuse by the leader and resentment in the subordinates.

This is cliché but it's true: *with great power comes great responsibility*.

On the other hand, influence is your ability to make people want to freely follow you.

Power

There are three sources of power and we will discuss them one by one.

- Legitimate Power

  It comes from an individual's position in an organization (or group). It is a source of power that cannot be questioned, like legal authority. To illustrate, if you break the law, cops have the legal authority to arrest you regardless of your status in society or even if your father has a position in the government. Legally, your father can't force the cop to drop the charges against you, not even if he is the president.

  Legitimate power rarely applies to alpha males, though you'll find some who are qualified to be classified as such. Alphas are generally *social leaders*, although they may have an authoritarian rule.

- Reward Power

  A leader can give rewards to their members for excelling at work or for their loyalty and obedience. Perfect examples in the business sector are salary increases, promotions, awards, or other incentives. Social rewards and recognitions are often given in the form of certificates and not as monetary rewards. These certificates serve as proof or affirmation of good deeds or outstanding work.

Alpha males may exercise this kind of power, though often not deliberately. They can do so as a result of who they actually are. Alpha males are recognized as some of the most sought-after people, thus their seal of approval is already seen as a great reward.

- Coercive Power

  This is the exact opposite of reward power. The leader resorts to threats and punishments to force their members to follow him. A perfect illustration of coercive power is when a father threatens to cut off his rebellious son if he (son) doesn't change.

  Alpha males will not be caught resorting to this kind of power. Coercive power should be the last resort, where position or rewards are not enough for a member to recognize one's leadership. This would be a desperate move, and alpha males are not desperate. They want their group to follow him in their own free will.

Influence

As for influence, it comes from charisma, expertise, and information.

We now know that charisma is a characteristic most alpha males possess that can help them get other people's approval and support. Leaders with charisma are seen as confident, passionate, good speakers, fun to be with, among others.

To be able to influence their group to act, a leader should show expertise on a particular subject matter. The group will be convinced to follow their leader if they see that he knows what he is doing.

To be a person of influence, he should possess the skills and specific competencies.

Charisma may get you the followers, but these followers will need an assurance that they made the right choice, so they consider your level of expertise and your competencies.

You cannot lead by example if you lack the knowledge of every subject that your followers might be interested in.

What Is More Important to Possess, Power or Influence?

Alpha males are socially dominant people, hence, they can easily influence others. This is the main reason why a lot of women would stay with the alpha males even if they are not rich, powerful, or popular (at least in terms of a political concept).

With influence, people will do whatever you want them to do without having the need to force them, they just do it out of respect and trust. Influence encourages loyalty, which makes people follow you even when you're not around.

The power that uses coercion for people to obey your commands will eventually lead to resentment. When your people will only follow you because they are afraid of you, you will not get the best effort from them. You cannot expect them to go the extra mile for you because, in the first place, they unwillingly obey you. This is not the kind of power and influence alpha males are known for.

Circumstances will require alpha males to apply coercive power to establish dominance, though. Again, this will be their last resort, when all else fails. This power might be applied when they need to handle a person who was caught harassing or threatening a member of their group, the alpha male leader will do everything in his power to protect the aggrieved party. In cases like this, the alpha male might resort to threats of punishment to the offender.

The alpha male, as a leader, uses influence to lead his people, and will only use power as his last resort.

Chapter 12: Alpha Male Rules of Seduction

In most cases, the alpha male doesn't have a hard time dating women. In fact, women would literally throw themselves over to the alpha males, short of offering themselves to the lucky alpha man.

But how does an alpha male attract women to date or spend the night with?

You may be good-looking and confident, but is she interested in you? Some women fancy alpha males. But men who seem mysterious are a challenge for them. The less a woman knows about you, the more attractive you are to her. They want to be the ones to discover your "secrets".

These are the simple rules to seduction a beautiful woman:

Create Sexual Tension – Flirt with Her

So, why flirt? It is important to create sexual tension between you and her because if not, you might get friend-zoned.

Women can be likened to a mirror. If you talk to her and treat her like a friend, then you will become her friend. But if you treat her like an attractive woman, you might become her lover. If you want to get intimate with a woman, then creating sexual tension is important.

There are two methods of flirting:

- Push-Pull

  The technique is simple: you "push" her away, either physically or emotionally, then let her come back in with the "pull". This can be verbal or nonverbal, it can even be a combination of both. It is effective because:

  > She is taken to an emotional rollercoaster ride, up and down, she cannot resist it;
  >
  > and it shows that you won't throw yourself at her feet.

  Push-pull flirting shows to her that you're not needy. It means that you like her but it's not a big deal if she likes you back. it appears that you are the one in control. You come off as the one trying to woo her, and not seeking to impress her.

- Chase Framing

  With this one, you'll playfully flirt, framing the interaction in such a way that *she* is the one chasing *you*. The innocent victim is you. She appears to be the one seducing you.

  A good illustration:

  > Woman: A good massage is always welcome.
  >
  > Man: I know what you're doing, are you seducing me by offering massages?

  Do you get the picture?

Flirting should be a fun activity. Go ahead and enjoy. Playfully tease her as if you were young children enjoying the playground.

Keep Physically Escalating

Some guys find themselves happy being with a woman and think that everything's going great. They feel they have a real connection and the feeling seems mutual. They go out on a date, and then nothing happens. After the third date, still, nothing intimate happens. In the end, the woman loses interest and simply disappears.

Most men make the same mistakes repeatedly – they fail to get intimate. They didn't try to escalate. Men have to take charge of intimacy. All you need to do is lead and she will follow.

For alpha males, this may not be a problem. They will always know how to escalate.

You simply approach her. Initiate the conversation and maintain that interaction. Get her number. Ask her out for a date. Remember, you lead she just follows. You're the man, you decide to escalate into the bedroom.

Continue Escalating

It all depends on you. continuously escalate. It's up to if your relationship would go forward.

From the moment you first meet her, you should be constantly escalating physically. If you don't do it, you'll just be wasting both of your time.

Start with a simple handshake or you may slightly touch her forearm or shoulder while you are talking, emphasizing a point.

Gradually escalate to flirting like pretending to be reading her palm like a fortune teller or playing with her fingers while singing, or shoving her then puller her closer to you.

Continue escalating. This time putting your arms around her or holding at her lower back as you guide her through a crowd. You may also begin resting your hand on her thigh or take a loose strand away from her face.

As you are escalating, pay attention to her body language, how she is reacting to your touch. Does she seem uncomfortable or she seems to be more receptive? Does she move away or does she respond and reciprocate?

If she's responding positively to your advances, continue your moves albeit cautiously watching for body language.

Move-in for a Kiss

As you continue escalating, you will eventually find yourself kissing, and then taking it to the next level.

How do you do it?

You slowly lean in while maintaining eye contact, looking at her lips for just a second, then going back to her eyes. Then, go for it!

Take note that you'll need some privacy to go for a kiss. Find a place where you two will be alone, like taking her home.

You'll also need to have some kind of physical familiarity since you have made light touches throughout the time you are together. Do not be afraid to make subtle touches.

If she suddenly feels awkward and turns away from you when you try to kiss her, simply brush it off. Just move on and resume with the conversation like nothing happened.

If she rejects your kiss, don't make it a big deal. Just move on.

But if you kiss and she responds, then there's only one thing that needs to be done.

Time to Seal the Deal

The moment you started kissing, the next step is obviously to have sex. So, you're having fun, simply tell her that you'd want to go somewhere private, and simply tell her that you'd like to get drinks at your place.

If she is into you, she's going to say yes.

Alternatively, if you're the one who was invited over to her place, the same applies. However, some women wouldn't want to be called sluts for giving in to sex on the first date. But if you make her feel that it is not the case, she'll begin to feel at ease and that she is ready for the next step.

The Final Escalation

So you're kissing, more passionately now. If you two ended up going to her apartment, she might be running around trying to get some drinks or looking for food, etc. Approach her gently from behind. Grab her by the hips. Get her closer. Breathe to her ear. Smell her. Kiss or even lightly brush her neck.

Then go for it!

Chapter 13: Alpha Male with Women

Throughout history, women have evolved. They are attracted to dominant alpha men – at least most of them – rather than Mr. Nice guys. However, some men are not considered alphas. The majority of alpha males learned to develop how to become alpha males.

For this chapter, use the information you can get from here as tools to help you attract women.

Take Charge and Lead

Alphas always want to be the dominant one, the one in charge. They always want to showcase their manliness. On the other hand, women want to feel feminine. They are more attracted to men who take charge and lead. They don't want to make all the decisions, like where they'll go and what they'll do. All they want is to be with a man who is confident and dominant.

Remember this: women feel sexy when they feel feminine.

You are the masculine, and she reciprocates as a feminine.

Be Confident

Women are turned off by neediness on the part of men. You can be handsome and rich, but if you're needy, then she won't ever be attracted to you. Men should be confident in their own skin. The alpha male is never insecure or defensive. They are not needy.

If you want unmatched sex appeal? Enhance your confidence, it's the most attractive trait man could possess. Confidence demonstrates that you are masculine, while neediness and insecurity demonstrate the opposite.

Act with Masculine Body Language

For a lot of people, they can tell whether a man is an alpha or not just by the way he walks, his posture, the way he talks, the way he holds himself, among others.

The alpha male will take up as much space as he wants. He is likely to lean back on his chair and rest an arm on the back of his chair.

His movements are slow and deliberate, not quick and uncontrolled.

Overall, he exudes calm authority.

Lift and Dress Well

A muscular body may make a man look more powerful and full of confidence, and women are actually biologically hardwired to feel a strong attraction for men who are powerful and confident. This is also true with a man who dresses well.

So, build those muscles and invest in nice clothes because you'll be perceived as confident and powerful, which will take you about 10 times more attractive to women.

Be Exciting, Mysterious, and Unpredictable

It's human nature to have a little inferiority complex. You notice a hot girl and you think about how awesome her life might be, and suddenly you feel inadequate.

Truth is, most hot girls live a regular, sometimes boring life, just like everyone else.

Just as guys often assume that hot girls lead exciting and adventurous lives (when in reality, they are just as ordinary as others), so do women. But women would do this a tad too far. This is the reason why women are more attracted to mysterious men. They would create a fantasy in their mind about these mysterious, dark men.

While this "mysterious, dark" man maybe just an ordinary guy who has a regular 9-5 job with a few friends, she is picturing him as some kind of a secret billionaire flirt who likes throwing wild parties. She would assume that when the man says he's busy, he is probably pursuing other girls.

Simply put, the less a woman knows about a man, the more attracted she becomes.

So, don't spill the beans all at once. Remain mysterious. Keep her wondering what you'll do next. Continue to be her mysterious yet exciting man.

Tease Her Playfully

Alpha males are not boring. They are provocative. They would tease women playfully.

For instance, if a girl asks an alpha man if she looks fat in her dress, he'll tell her that she looks like she's gained 200 pounds and that she should take that dress off at once, along with undies – then winks at her.

The alpha male is not a woman's shoulder to cry. He is there to have fun.

So, don't hesitate to tease women, then have fun with them.

Chapter 14: Alpha Male in Relationship

Alpha males like things in a certain way. They want a partner with whom they can feel masculine. But they are not the easiest to read in terms of showing their love to the people they love. When it comes to their feelings, they are not the best communicators so it would be up to their partner to decode their actions.

The alpha male will always look for a non-alpha female. They always want to be the dominant one in their relationships. They'd like to feel superior.

This chapter includes a list of how alpha males show their love.

How an Alpha Male Shows Love

He will constantly put his arms around his woman.

They are actually unaware of this gesture. It is just automatic when they are with the woman they love. All they want is to protect her and one way of expressing that is by putting an arm around her.

It is also a way of making their territory, especially if they are in public. It's like saying, *this girl is mine and no other guy should try to take her from him.*

He talks about a future together.

Alpha males are not too good at expressing themselves when it comes to love. They are not even someone who says *I love you* often. They'll just express that in ways they alone can do.

The alpha male would often discuss a future with the one they love. It is a good sign if he talks about being with her in the future.

He would put down other men.

It is in the nature of alpha males to feel that they are the top dog. If their self-esteem is being shaken a little, they will find a way to put other men down. If he loves a woman and he sees her talking to another guy, notice how they will try to put down that guy his woman is talking to. He will resort to belittling the other guy. That is how he marks his territory.

She should expect him to empty the trash.

Yes, he'll take the trash out for the woman he loves. This is one way of showing their affection towards her. They see things as a man's job and they will immediately jump into doing it. it's the simple things that should mean a lot.

He is extremely passionate.

He will make a woman feel he loves her by being extremely passionate in bed. Alpha males are sensual lovers and they will make sure that their partner's needs are met.

He will always look at his woman with a burning passion, ready to "devour" her.

He would constantly walk her home.

They always express their love by making sure their partner is safe and protected. If they are not yet living with their partner, they would make it a point to walk her home after a date. They may also ask to stay over just so they can look after the woman they love.

This is something that most 21st Century women couldn't quite understand. But they have to realize that the alpha males have good intentions in doing this.

He will call her to make sure she is okay.

If he is not with the woman they love, they would constantly call her just to ask how she is. This is an alpha male being protective and loving.

He is chivalrous.

A few men would open doors in this modern society. But the alpha male would still be opening doors for others, not just for their partners. They would still pull a chair for her. It's their way of making things easier for her every little way they can.

He would get up as she leaves the table.

He would still do this in this modern society. It's a sign of respect and shows that he is attentive to whatever she is doing. You'll not see this often in most men but the alpha male still does this to the woman they love.

He'll get mad when other people make her upset.

By now we know that the alpha male is extremely protective of the woman they love, and they will do so at all costs. If he hears another person lashing out at her or hurting her feelings, he will get angry at the situation and at the person who would do this.

They can be sweet but when he sees that the woman he loves is upset, he will do everything to ease her pain.

He gets her suitcase.

Whenever they can, the alpha male will carry a woman's suitcase. They may also help her carry a lot of grocery bags. They will try to make life easier for the woman they love.

He is reliable with some of the practical matters around the house.

They don't have qualms about doing odd jobs around the house. They will simply be happy to change the lightbulbs for her. They'll fix a leaking faucet. They'll just always be there to lend a helping hand to their partner.

The alpha male is physical in bed.

He will scoop her out of the couch and carry her to the bedroom to make love to her. This is a demonstration of their own strength.

Chapter 15: How to Be Awesome

The word *awesome* is defined in the dictionary as *inspiring awe*.

Why settle to just being good when you can be awesome? You're an alpha male, that's a good start. You are already being given the proper respect and admiration. Something awesome will make people stop and take notice.

To be awesome, you simply have to be you.

This is a simple guide.

It's a way of life. It's how you behave and how you interact with the world. It's all about putting yourself and what you have to offer into the world.

Examples of Being Awesome

- Having a positive outlook in life.

- Being an optimist.

- Living out your dreams.

- Leading by example.

- Helping other people any way you can.

- Giving back to the community.

- Treating other people with kindness and respect.

- Having the courage to stand up, not just for himself but for others.

- Being a man with high morals.

Be Awesome

To be awesome, you only have to be you. Here's how you become awesome:

- Set big goals.

  If you already have set goals for yourself, revisit them. To be awesome, you have to be daring with your goals. Set up audacious goals. Just do your thing!

- "Upgrade" your mojo.

  Increase your mojo by:

  > *being true to yourself,*
  > *setting yourself up to small but frequent wins,*
  > *feed your soul – positive things.*

- Increase your gumption.

  If your "mojo" has a "friend", it will be gumption. It is that friend who gets all the hard blows, but continues to stay motivated, continues to hope, has the courage, and enthusiasm to keep on going in life.

- Don't entertain self-doubt.

  It's human nature to have self-doubts sometimes. But as an alpha male, you shouldn't entertain those thoughts and just continue being awesome.

- Learn more skills.

  When you're an alpha, it doesn't mean that you know it all. Surely, there are things that you could learn to do. You just have to find what interests you.

- Continue to be physically active.

  To be awesome, you should continue being fit. You'll feel good and you'll look even better.

- You just got to have that passion burning.

  Continue to be passionate about everything.

- Be kind.

  Alpha males are known to be strong individuals, but they are also kind and gentle when they need to. They are full of compassion.

How awesome do you feel right now?

Live the life you deserve!

Chapter 16: Habits You Should Develop to Become an Alpha Male

In this chapter, you'll know more habits of alpha males that you can develop to become one.

Conquer Your Fears

To be an alpha male you have to learn to live your life to the fullest.

Alpha males have masted conquering their fears of the unknown. They have learned to embrace discomfort just to pursue something they are passionate about. They know there will be challenges in the pursuit of their goals, but they are still willing to do it.

Write down the things about life that you're afraid of. Consider every area where fear is holding you back from living your life to the fullest.

Probably you've become overweight and you're afraid that people will ridicule you when you go to the gym. Or maybe you are stuck in a toxic relationship but you're afraid that if you get out of it you'll never find another woman to love again.

Whatever it is, write it down. When you're done, ask yourself these questions:

> *What could be the worst thing that could happen?*
> *What could be the best thing that might happen?*
> *If I fail, how long does will it take until I'm back on my feet?*

You'd be surprised that when you think about what you were afraid of, the worst outcomes may not be as bad as you thought they would.

Get out of that comfort zone and live!

Don't Let Anyone Tell You What Path to Take

Alpha males have a clear vision and purpose. They know what they want to do with their lives. That is how they are inspiring others. They know what they want and they don't let others dictate to them where they should go to pursue their goals.

Chart your own path, then take action. Fulfill your destiny.

Aim for Constant Progress

For alpha males, their true competition is themselves. They will never get caught wallowing in self-pity because other people are more successful than him. They don't compare themselves with other people.

Success may not yet have come to them just yet but they know that small successes will eventually bring them to their ultimate goal.

So, don't worry if your life is not as good as your friends. Success in life doesn't happen in an instant. It's a process and you have to go through the process in order to appreciate your success more.

Don't Argue Just Because

Alpha males believe in action and learning rather than starting a disagreement. They wouldn't waste their time arguing about their beliefs, religion, philosophy, and politics on the internet or with their circle of friends. Instead, they are committed to taking action on the things that that they know will help improve themselves.

This doesn't mean that you should shy away from intelligent discussions and debates. The key is to agree to disagree.

Do Good Because it is the Right Thing to Do

We've said this over and over in the book, alpha males are kind and have the deepest desire to do good. But they are not doing this because they want to become popular, but simply because they are good people.

They help people without expecting anything in return.

They have genuine compassion and empathy for others.

They believe that the only thing that matters is the impact you had on other people.

When you wake up in the morning every day, ask yourself this question, *What good can I do today?*

Always Speak Your Truth

When alpha males believe in something, they won't hesitate to defend that belief.

The alpha male speaks his mind, but still with respect for others. They will not back down from anything they believe in. While he may respect the opinions of other people, he will not be controlled by these opinions.

Speak your mind even if other people might shut you down. Be brave enough to stake a stand.

Develop Self-Reliance

The alpha male is his own man. He cultivates self-reliance. He knows he has the power to make his own choices because they know it is the best option.

But to be self-reliant doesn't mean you shouldn't ask for help from friends or neighbors. There will be instances when you need to admit that you need help.

Build a Strong Body

You don't have to have six-pack abs or 20" biceps to be considered an alpha male. However, you should be both physically and emotionally fit so you can build a strong body. You have a responsibility to yourself and to others to take care of your well-being.

You can't live life to the fullest if your body is not strong and healthy.

You Should Know How to Defend Yourself

To be able to defend yourself you have to be physically fit, so this ties back to the last habit. Every man should learn to fight at some point. Little self-defense techniques would suffice, though.

Take Care of Yourself

Self-care is important, especially if you're an alpha male. Your well-being should be a top priority.

Start with one act of self-care a day. You may try meditation. Or one day you can try to do something you enjoy doing, like a hobby. Go to a sauna or get a massage.

So, don't neglect your health.

Live By Your Values

You should live by your own code. Define your values and live by them. Live with integrity.

Most people develop depression and anxiety because they are living a life that is not aligned with their values.

Don't say your family is important yet you spend more time working. To have a happy family life, you should spend time with them.

Do you want to be happy? Then all that you do, all that you say, and all that you think should be aligned with one another.

Establish what's important to you. If it's family, then go for it. If it's financial success, then pursue it. If it is to go on an adventure on your own, then go. You don't become less of an alpha male if you pursue these things.

Be True to Your Word

Your word is your honor so you have to keep it. If you say you'll do something, then do it. If you say you won't do it, then don't. That's a straightforward principle.

Keeping your word gains the trust of the people who follow you. Your reputation would also be good. But most importantly, you learn to trust yourself.

Your words are important so use them wisely.

Failing to live up to your word will become easier for you to lose conviction. Whatever you say won't have an impact anymore because no one will believe you if you keep on failing at your promise.

You're human, you get exhausted, so don't spread yourself thin. Give promises that you know you can keep. If you are unsure then do not commit. It's better to say "no" early than to break your promise later on because you didn't have the luxury of time.

In this modern world, it's hard to find a man who remains true to their word no matter the circumstances.

Don't be one of those men.

Master the Art of Charm, Attraction, and Seduction

You've already learned the art of seduction and being charismatic in the previous chapters.

You should be able to attract certain types of people who can help you to achieve your goals. Likewise, you should also find a woman with whom you can build a family with, if settling down is one of your main goals.

Improving your confidence would help boost your charisma.

Make Your Life Harder, Taste Sweet Victory Later

You have to understand that alpha males do not hope to make an easy life, their main goal is to grow not to live in luxury and comfort.

They know that the challenges and adversity they'll encounter will make them stronger. These will help build their character and teach them to be resilient. Make the uncomfortable your new comfort.

You Have to be Willing to Die for Something You Believe in

Alpha males are willing to die for anything and anyone they love. They will die fighting for their family, their honor, to defend their values, etc.

Becoming an alpha male is no mean feat. It's a journey, it doesn't happen overnight.

You might have to encounter discomfort and hardships or suffer pain, but in the end, it will be worth it.

Chapter 17: Secret Tricks that Will Make You More of an Alpha Immediately

Most men want to be alpha males because they want to take control of their lives and the lives of the people they care about.

We have compiled a few secret tricks to make you an alpha male in an instant.

Sound Like an Alpha Male

To become an alpha male, start with your voice. Alpha males speak with confidence, at a relaxed pace, and with a low and controlled pitch. You'll never hear them rush with their words.

The key is to be confident and it will show in your voice.

Don't Worry About What Others are Up To

They are not competitive – they don't want to compete with other men just to show who is more superior. In fact, alpha males support each other. And they don't like drama. That's what separates them from other personality types.

Don't Be Passive

These men are assertive -they are not afraid to speak their minds. And when they open their mouths, they don't speak empty words, they make it a point that they are knowledgeable enough.

There is No Comfort Zone – Take Risks

It doesn't exist because they live for adventure. They are not afraid to take on new challenges. For them, there's nothing that cannot be done.

They are the leader of the pack, they will never lead their pack into danger, hence, they will be the first ones to do something. That is how they mitigate the risks to protect their pack.

Be Nice, But Not Too Nice

Being nice to people is a good thing. But you can't be too nice as other people might take advantage of you. An alpha male is assertive. You don't have to try to be nice all the time, but you should not be a pushover either.

Be Good, But Only When Needed

To put this in the proper context, you shouldn't show off your good deeds all the time. Just let your goodness flow naturally. It should be a habit and not a mere superficial act.

Be Discreet When Giving Praise

If someone is doing a good job, acknowledge it, but remember to be discreet about it. If you just throw away appreciating remarks all the time, your words will soon lose their impact. Make them strive for your appreciation, don't give it away freely. Show your appreciation when you really mean it, and not because it is expected of you.

Never Lash Out When You're Angry

Alpha males always act so coolly, do they ever get angry? Yes, they do, but they do not act out of impulse. They know how to handle their emotions. They will try to cool down first, then they will analyze the situation, and finally, they'll act.

Ask for Whatever You Want

If you want something, all you have to do is ask.

> *Ask someone to go on a date.*
> *Ask for money.*
> *Ask for discounts.*
> *Ask for contact numbers.*
> *Ask for a job.*
> *Ask for favors.*

You wouldn't know if you can if you don't try. Most people are far too intimidated to ask for what they want. They prefer the nice guys because they don't want others to think that is arrogant, greedy, or imposing. But you are just being assertive and true.

Love Yourself

Believe in yourself, love yourself. We are only limited by the limitations we put on ourselves. It's an adage quote, but it is true – what you think, you will manifest. So, what better way to enhance your confidence by first loving yourself.

Believe that you are an interesting guy, that you a good person, that women are easily drawn to you, among others. You got the picture.

Be "attracted to yourself". Fix whatever you can fix, but learn to accept those that are beyond your control.

Think positive so you'll attract positive energy.

A Funny Guy is an Attractive Guy

There is a thin line between being funny and acting like a clown. Surely, a woman wouldn't want a clown. Your people at work naturally wouldn't allow a clown to lead them.

Humor is a good thing and it makes a man attractive for never would be a dull moment with them.

Bonus Chapter: The Alpha Checklist

This last chapter summarizes the traits, characteristics, and principles for the alpha discussed in this book.

The Law of Manliness

1. Men should be self-reliant.

2. To achieve success and happiness, you have to work for it.

3. You have to create your own path.

4. Practice self-denial and forget instant gratification.

5. Continue to fight, even when you know you are to lose, just fight.

6. Be accountable.

7. Don't worry if you should fall, worry if you don't even try.

8. Be kind but don't let people take advantage of you.

9. Always be fair.

10. Never allow injustice.

11. Develop a habit of and love for reading.

12. Take time off weekly.

13. It's all right to laugh, especially at yourself.

14. Don't be too dependent on the internet.

15. Basic manners are always in style.

16. Treat people fairly.

17. Let your actions do the talking.

18. Money isn't everything. Find life's meaning.

19. Make the best of any situation.

Characteristics of an Alpha Male

1. A deep and confident voice

2. Good looking

3. Medium built

4. Maintains eye contact

5. Physically fit

6. Manly body language

7. Confident

8. Touchy

9. Calm

10. Doesn't need external validation

11. Has growth potential

12. Good problem solver

13. Fearless

14. Ambitious

15. Passionate

16. Humble

17. With high moral ground

18. Does not make a conscious effort to be an alpha

Developing Physical and External Confidence

1. Be physically fit

2. Follow proper diet

3. Create your personal fashion style

4. Good grooming

Acting and Communicating Confidently

1. Positive attitude

2. Positive body language

3. Good verbal communication

4. Acting a true gentleman

5. Don't let criticisms stop you

Living Confidently

1. Pursue happiness
2. Be likable
3. Gain other people's trust and respect
4. Never entertain self-doubt
5. Excel in your career

Character Traits to Develop

1. Be courageous
2. Easily controls emotion
3. Has a purpose in life
4. Make decisions and stand by them
5. Not afraid to speak his mind
6. Not governed by rules
7. Stay fit
8. Not afraid to say no, does it with kindness
9. Recognize own weaknesses and find ways to improve them
10. Good posture
11. Be passionate

Develop Charisma

1. Alpha males feel strong emotions
2. They can compel people to feel the same emotion

3. He is his own man

4. Makes others feel good about themselves

How to Be a Good Leader

Find the balance between power and influence. Use your influence to make others follow you, and use power as a last resort. Lead by example.

Rules of Seduction

1. Create sexual tension – flirt with her

2. Keep physically escalating

3. Build up for a kiss

4. Move-in for that kiss

5. Seal the deal in bed

Alpha Male with Women

1. Take charge and lead. Women want dominant men who are sure about themselves.

2. Be confident but not needy. Women don't want their men clingy and needy.

3. Develop masculine body language – calm authority.

4. Make sure to stay fit.

5. Dress well.

6. Be exciting. Be mysterious. Be unpredictable. Keep her guessing all the time.

7. Tease her playfully.

How an Alpha Male Shows Love

1. He will constantly put his arms around his woman.
2. He talks about the future with her.
3. He puts down other men who are interested in his girl.
4. He'll empty the trash for her.
5. He is extremely passionate.
6. He will make sure to walk her home.
7. He will call just to make sure she's okay.
8. He is chivalrous.
9. He gets up when she leaves the table.
10. He helps her carry her bag, even if she doesn't ask him to.
11. He is reliable.
12. He is passionate in bed.

How to be Awesome

1. Set big goals
2. Upgrade your mojo
3. Increase your gumption
4. Don't entertain self-doubt
5. Learn more skills
6. Continue being physically active
7. Keep the passion burning

8. Be kind, always

Habits to Develop to be an Alpha Male

1. Conquer your fears. Take risks.

2. Don't let anyone tell you what path to take.

3. Aim for constant progress.

4. Don't argue just because. Don't start a senseless disagreement.

5. Do good because it is the right thing to do.

6. Always speak the truth.

7. Develop self-reliance, but remember it is okay to ask for help from family and friends if you need them.

8. Build a strong body.

9. Know how to defend yourself.

10. Take care of yourself.

11. Live by your values.

12. Be true to your word.

13. Master the art of charm, attraction, and seduction.

14. Make life harder, taste the sweet victory later.

15. You have to be willing to die for something you believe in.

Secret Tricks that Will Make You an Alpha Male Immediately

1. Sound like an alpha male – deep, confident voice.

2. Don't worry about what others are up to.

3. Don't be passive.

4. There is no comfort zone, you have to learn to take risks.

5. Be nice, but too nice, lest you want to be a pushover.

6. Be good only when needed. You don't have to let the world know of every good deed you do.

7. Be discreet when giving praise. Show appreciation only when you mean it. Your words lose their impact when you give praise for everything they do.

8. Never lash out when you're angry. Cooldown first because you act.

9. Ask for whatever you want, that's not being demanding, but being assertive and sure of yourself.

10. Love yourself. Believe in yourself.

11. A funny guy is an attractive guy.